The Foolish Risks of God

The Foolish
Risks of God

Michael Ball

MOWBRAY
London and New York

Mowbray
A Continuum imprint
The Tower Building, 11 York Road, London SE1 7NX
370 Lexington Avenue, New York NY 10017-6503
www.continuumbooks.com

First published 2002

British Library Cataloguing-in-Publication Data
A catalogue record for this book is available from the British Library.

ISBN 0–8264–6395–9

Typeset by RefineCatch Limited, Bungay, Suffolk
Printed and bound by Biddles Ltd, www.biddles.co.uk

Contents

How to read this Book

Books and stories can be adventures, gates to lands of heart and mind, gardens, medicine chests, paths to the future, revelations of the past. They can be guides and warnings, informative and mysterious. They can be taken anywhere both in mind and hand, and have been used for building and destroying people and nations for thousands of years. Biblical parables illustrate all these categories and a lot more besides. The parables have passed into common parlance. They have been used as moral weapons, as social and environmental examples, blasted in scaremongering ways from pulpit and soap box, or gently unravelled as pictures of the nature of God. They can be roughly popped into types, genera, for instance, parables of the Kingdom, parables of judgement, and so on, and although lumpings of this kind are partially helpful, in many ways parables defy being put into a box, and leap into another one as soon as the academic paperweight is removed.

They are in all sorts of ways problematic to scholars, but problematic in a wonderfully exciting way. New excitements are constantly being revealed about them, and they are as thrilling for the digger as any archaeological site and for much the same reasons. Little bits can lead to unexpected treasures. They are the stories of the New Testament which stay with former Sunday School pupils and sufferers of dry religious education classes, long after other portions of Scripture have disappeared from memory. For many people parables are their picture of Jesus.

Besides that, they contain within them all the ordinary problems and possibilities of life and loving, the difficulties and joys of our relationships one with another and with God. The deepest problems of the universe are hidden in their simplicity, whether it be free will and choice, reward and punishment, or justice and mercy, power and powerlessness, and in most cases Jesus has complete confidence in our ability to understand their significance for ourselves, despite what the Gospel writers and preachers ever since have tried to do with them. They are not commandments for behaviour, though they may gently persuade, neither are they black and white morsels of theology. They are signposts to God and guides to living and loving.

Like many of the parables this is very much a pick-and-mix book. Readers may begin anywhere and move backwards and forwards as they please. It is not an academic study of parables, though I am very grateful to such scholars as C. H. Dodd, Joachim Jeremias, and Christopher Evans. In some chapters I have hardly analysed the parable at all but barefacedly used it as a frame for thoughts arising from the story. In some cases those thoughts are at some distance from the usual interpretation of the parable. I justify this with the argument that in Jewish thinking an enormous range of thoughts, stories, short picture-sayings, diverse proverbial snippets, and even a very few words indeed, were classed as parables, or having the nature of parable. 'I am the door' is hardly a story, but for the Rabbi it would have been thought of as a parable.

The first chapter is about some of the characteristics of parables, but I haven't worked these through in all the parables I have written about. Readers can perhaps do that for themselves. In most cases I have divided the chapter up into preliminary thoughts and then a discussion of the parable itself, but in others the thinking runs continuously. The length of the chapter has no relationship to the length of the parable.

What should be the main qualities of a Lent book? Tentative suggestions might be, first, that it should stimulate fresh thinking on subjects associated with the Cross and Passion. Why was such an excruciating means of salvation necessary and what does it tell us about the nature of God? And for me some of the clues to both those areas of thought are the parables. I realize that my thinking about all this, particularly on forgiveness and punishment, is not that of large numbers of Christian folk. But I would hope that my thoughts might stimulate Lent groups to throw such matters about with vigour, passion and cheerfully open minds.

Secondly, down the ages the Passion, as well as being the main subject for Christian art, has also been the principal theme for meditation and thoughtful prayer, mostly personal but often in public as well. Many churches have a Lent service such as Compline, where there is an address attached which opens up the Cross and Passion.

Again, I hope some of the chapters might be useful to be developed for such services.

I have tried, therefore, to come at many of the parables slantwise, to give different possibilities for such thinking. In some cases I have tried to talk about them in parables, but that may be just another name for riddles.

Thirdly, this book is scattered with words and phrases such as 'perhaps', 'probably', 'it seems to me', 'possibly'. The vast majority of Christian thinking, even credal and moral thinking, I suggest, should be approached as if it were still open to fresh thinking and possible change. Sentences I have heard fairly often in my ministry such as 'This is what it means and that's the end of the matter', or 'This is right and that is wrong and the sooner people realize this the better', or even 'I know what I think on this matter and I am absolutely clear about it, thank you', are both limiting and misleading. Jesus told many of his parables to loosen attitudes of this kind. I happen to think that is what a Lent book should do as well. And this is what the Cross and Passion should do to our attitudes about out faith.

There are phrases attached to parables, or parts of the parables themselves, that I do not think came from the lips of our Lord, or if they did they are in the wrong place. The evidence for this falls into three categories. First, that of various characteristics in the style of writing and use of words. Secondly, what we know about the agenda of the early Church. They are using the lips of Jesus to plug their own line. Thirdly, where the parables seem to me to be out of tune with the personality and thinking of Jesus as portrayed by the Gospels. Clearly his thinking and personality developed, that was part of his normal humanity, but even allowing for that it is almost impossible to believe that such phrases are dominical. One has to ask whether they are in tune with his revealing of the nature of God as seen elsewhere in the Gospels. Different people, however, have different views about the nature of God and the personality of Jesus, and would have no hesitation about attributing such statements to our Lord. Jesus was a man of his time and I may be in all this judging those bits and pieces by my twenty-first century standards.

Finally, I find the parables entertaining. They often have the quality of a 'have you heard the one about . . .' type of story. One of them is pathos all the way through (The Vineyard and the Owner's Son) but the entertainment in many of the 'serious' ones comes from the mental pictures they create. They reflect the playful nature of our

Lord and his gift of mixing teasing humour and a penetrating depth of thinking. Not a gift we find in the writers of the Epistles.

So, Q. Will this book make it clear what a parable is?

A. I suspect, almost hope, not. But I do hope that it will enable people to see parables in daily life and use those and the parables of old to explore the nature of God.

Q. Will the meaning of the parables be more clear after reading this book?

A. Again I both hope so and hope not. My wish is that readers should do exactly what Christ advised his listeners to do, take the parables away and work out their meaning for themselves. My hope is that some of the material in this book will be helps and starting-points for them to do so.

Above all I would like readers to use what they have worked out for themselves and see how it applies to that display of the nature of God seen in the Cross and Passion of his Son.

1

Introduction

The Parables and the Passion

At first sight and sound many of the parables seem as straightforward as children's stories, games or nursery rhymes. There is a treasure-hunt parable, for instance. There are stories in which good triumphs and sometimes where the bad are made exceedingly uncomfortable. Then, there are stories where there is an oddity and a twist about the ending, where the unexpected leaves us wondering. The very telling of the parables breathes a simplicity, almost an innocence, at times. They leave us smiling, crying or puzzled, as are children by those other ancient tales.

Like those rhymes or tales for the young, parables can be very short, just a sentence or two, or they can be an extended story, often in some way or other incomplete, but arresting and worth endless repetition. They are 'tell it again' stories where children would ask 'Did the elder brother come to the party after all?' 'What happened to the rich man's brothers in the end?' They depend for their effect on imagination and verbal pictures, just as those early rhymes and stories do. Like them the parables are full of colours, full of emotion, sometimes quite exquisite miniatures, sometimes splashings on a large canvas.

But like those rhymes and tales we knew word for word when young, the simplicity skin of the parables covers other treasures below. They are onion and globe artichoke stories. They invite us to peel off the layers. They cry out for exploration. For instance, many nursery rhymes have a history. Mary, Mary quite contrary, is Mary Tudor. 'Four and Twenty Blackbirds', Henry VIII and the monasteries. So with the parables. As we shall see, many of them are perhaps based on either older stories, or local ones, or those currently circulating in the 'Galilee Gazette'. They often arose it seems out of the current situation, as did those tales of childhood. They were immediate to mind and memory and also take-away stories.

Like those nursery tales and verses the parables often have obvious or hidden signs and symbols in them. The silver bells and cockle shells refer to the Sanctus bell in the Mass, and the shell to baptism. So in the parable of the Prodigal Son each of the father's gifts on his return may have symbolic meaning. The parables reward us continually with secret excitements.

One other point in this comparison of childhood literature and parables. Nursery rhymes and stories were, and probably still are, often used as moral tales by those who tell them. 'So you see, dear, they got rid of the monks and monasteries' when the 'Four and Twenty Blackbirds' had been recited. No doubt some would add their own opinion such as 'So very sad and wicked of the king', or 'A good thing too. They were a greedy lot', depending on which school of thought the reciter belonged to. Likewise the Church at a very early stage added explanations or little moral dicta to make certain their readers knew the accepted thinking. More of that later.

In other words, the thrill of the parables is unending. We soon realize in studying them that the search is continuous. One clue leads to another. The more we prod around and dissect them, the more we discover. I need hardly say that the divine nature is almost totally ungraspable, inexpressible, real but intangible, and can best be told in the painting and music of story. We can magnify the colours and sounds of those paintings and musical scores by our study and devotion, but behind it all is something that penetrates heart and mind, yet ever escapes us. Seen in parts, but most of it, iceberg-like, is hidden from our scholarly or prayerful gaze, though its presence is solidly there. Like scientific study, like most research, the more you reveal the more there is to be unravelled.

So let me make first of all a few general remarks about the characteristics of parables, which are the objects of this Lenten chase, characteristics found in all the Gospels, and then apply them briefly to the Passion which is in itself, as is all the incarnate life, a living parable, a human story behind which lurks the nature of God, the exploring of which, the research of which, is the most thrilling thing we can do and encounter.

I feel more strongly than I can say that the exploration of the nature of God is a prime activity of humanity. An exploration encountered in our daily lives and jobs, in our homes and enjoyments, in all we do, but most of all in worship, in prayer, word and sacrament. It is seen too in what the scientists call the stimulus bombardment of our minds and hearts and souls, in the face of a child and an old person and in all the joys of creation. And that exploration is where, it seems to me, our Christian life must begin. There is a strong tendency, nowadays as ever, to see the Christian life primarily in terms of the issues of morality, and often hard-line morality at that. 'He died to make us good', as Mrs Alexander puts it in a famous Passiontide hymn.

But as history shows, nasty things happen if you begin with issue-morality and codes of conduct, and nasty things happen particularly to the proclaimers and inevitably to the enforcers of those codes of morality, however much they are based on passages of Scripture.

If we begin, however, by exploring the nature of God as seen in our Lord, his parables, and in particular the parable of his death and Passion, unconditional mercy, unconditional forgiveness and unconditional love may stand a chance. Unconditional grace may come top of the list in this exploration, and our response to that grace something God longs for, but whatever our response, the outpouring of the benefits of his Passion is not dependent on that response, I would contend. It is the excitement, the awe, the amazement that this divine exploration arouses that in the end, through grace, will 'convert' and spill over into goodness, which the hunt for the treasures of God produces. I have seen even tough old bishops use a Kleenex tissue when talking of such mysteries of God's nature. Parables are some of the scents we follow in the hunt, scents still alive with the smell of the hare of God we chase, but which has always moved on though always leaving us clues to his presence. Lent, perhaps, is the time when the chase becomes hottest, our senses alerted by the disciplines and discipleship by which we train ourselves.

The Parables

A few characteristics, then, of parables that entrance me. Not theological ones, but ones that for me light up the nature of God and his creation. They also light up the nature of humanity, revealing not only what we are but what we can become.

Beauty first. St Luke may be the leading composer in this field but all Gospel writers have an amazing knack, a planned and trained skill with the verbal brush. A few strokes of that brush and we are there in the hills with the Sower, on the road from Jerusalem to Jericho, plotting with the Unjust Steward. Every little word is a colour on the canvas, and where we used to think that Mark was a crude writer superseded by Matthew and Luke, scholars now realize that there is a superb minimalist pathos in his painting that artists of that school would be proud of. The appeal of beauty is at the heart of the parables and, as I hope to describe, at the heart of the Passion too.

Secondly, risk. There is an alarming, stupid risk in so many of the parables. The parable of the Vineyard for instance, which we will look at in detail in another chapter. Madness, after the servants have been beaten and mugged to send your only son, and hope all will be well. The risk of commending the Unjust Steward when he has robbed you of your rights. Let alone the Prodigal Son where every stage of the story is laden with risk. Scripture itself is a book that might be entitled 'The Foolish Risks of God', and God surrounds our redemption with risks to his divinity, risks which are hidden in so many of the parables Jesus told.

Thirdly in my list of parable characteristics comes open-endedness. In all probability they were never stories where meaning and morals were neatly tied up at the end. I remember the relief I felt when our headmaster, who taught us Divinity for School Certificate, suggested that what is to me a tedious explanation of the parable of the Sower was probably not part of the parable as told by Jesus. We could forget all that allegorical stuff about what every sort of soil represented. They, he contended, were added on by the early Church which like the later one only wanted people to think in the way they approved of. Our headmaster may have been having a Bultmannesque morning, of course, but it lightened my schoolboy heart that I could throw the parable around for myself, apply it to different situations, or not apply it to anything at all and just know and feel its truth.

Let me go down another autobiographical path for a while, to even earlier years, when my brother and I were in a boarding house for eleven-year-olds. It was run by two massive Methodist matrons. One was a vegetarian who enjoyed chicken and sausages and the other one toyed from time to time with the Church of England. What other cracks were there in their respectable armour, we wondered. But they were supremely good at telling stories about real situations. Parables, in fact. For a while we were mesmerized, but we all turned off and thought eleven-year-old thoughts when the moral principle was drawn out of the story. The whole atmosphere was spoilt. We were not Victorian children. For me the joy of a parable is its openness, its 'take this away and roll it round the taste-buds of your mind, heart and soul'. That's where the excitement and nourishment lie.

No, parables do not preach at you, they do not in a sense even teach you; they persuade your inner self of something that is often indefinable but lies, I suspect, near the heart of God. They are an open gate leading through to a place not of conduct or morality, but beyond them to something that changes men and women almost without their realizing that such a process is happening. They are grace-bearing, and open-ended grace at that.

Just one more thing. Very often it seems our Lord taught, preached, and 'parabled' on the sea-shore. He looked up and saw a sower sowing on a hill nearby. He saw fishermen in their boats hauling in their nets and spoke of judgement in the picture language of sorting out the catch. He stood on the resurrection-shore and fed his disciples in mind and body. Somehow or other that place between land and sea, the shore, speaks of a joining, an exploring of both the reality of the land and the mystery of the sea's depths. For the Jews the seas were a place of dread. St John in the Revelation looks forward to the time when there will be no more sea. It was a place of unknowns compared with the firmness and visibility of the land. Parables are sea-shore stories. They link together and yet are part of both: the reality in the story itself, and yet the mystery that is behind it. They are often dangerous tales as well as mysterious ones, as far as usual straightforward theological thinking is concerned. They dare to say things that challenge the ordinary theology of Jesus's time adding the unthinkable to that theology. They link real things to the depths of mystery. The shore is a parable of the nature of parable.

The Passion

A brief reconnoitre before I go on to an exploration of individual parables and their Passion content. A reconnoitre of how I see the Passion in the light of the characteristics I have just described.

Beauty, to begin with. Strangely enough, perhaps, there is an inner artistry and beauty about the whole Passion narrative. This must be so, as God is giving us his masterpiece through his Son. A masterpiece of story, of reality, of mystery. Not the beauty of a Mona Lisa or a nativity scene, (though for many of the characters in the Passion there is the beauty of a different kind of birth) but a beauty that tears the heart and mind and startles with truth. A word that meant much the same as 'real' to the Greeks. A beauty that changes throughout the narrative with moments of warmth and hospitality as Jesus puts his feet up at Bethany in the first evenings of the week, to the agonized beauty of 'The Scream' both of Jesus and all humanity as seen in the Passiontide story. A beauty of poetry in some of the phrases Jesus uses, to the women of Jerusalem, for instance. The beauty of the Lord's nakedness, however shaming to a Jew, which restores parabolically the innocence of Eden.

In ancient languages, I am assured, beauty often means something that is fitting, apt, ripe or blooming. Such is the beauty of the Cross. It does things in the same way as the beauty of a parable does. It appeals in the way that a striking and skilful poster does, though in the end its beauty can only be expressed perhaps in the parables of art, music, poetry and drama; the Phineas Fletcher hymn for instance 'Drop, drop slow tears and bathe those beauteous wounds', or in the music of the St. Matthew Passion. All the beauty of parable, its telling, its construction, its appeal, its skill, its twisting of heart and mind, are there in the Cross and Passion and all that is behind so many of the actual parables as well.

And much the same can be said of my second characteristic of parables – risk. A characteristic of God which he passes on in full measure to his Son. The Cross is the ultimate daring. I take the line that Mark has got it right. In the Marcan risk everything goes. There are no interpolations that make us think that Jesus knew it would all be resurrected the other side of the grave. No tender stories of the penitent thief, or the caring for his mother and St John. There is a total blackness that the other Gospel writers writing after Mark could not cope with and added bits, it seems, to make the story more gentle. Even down to such little changes, as John Fenton points out, where the dead body of Jesus is described by the others in the softer word, body, while in Mark, the dead Jesus is a corpse. Dead and that's that. Only hints of resurrection follow. The early Marcan narrative makes it clear that all the confidence of Jewish theology is put at risk and vanishes. Vindication, God-upholding, loyalty of friends, followers and family also – risked and in the end collapses. It is a parable that dares all without a hint of possible triumph. Risk is painted in the earliest Gospel as total night without a hint of dawn, except the fear of the early visitors to the tomb.

Beauty and risk in the Passion. But there is daring open-endedness there as well. It is not all tied up and followed through though it is complete in its attainment of our salvation. St Paul makes that incompleteness clear at times, mysteriously clear, in his letters, and St John meditates on it in his writings. The Passion is the fulfilling of Scripture but has to be fulfilled in the work of the Church. There is also in every life a working out of the Passion to be done. The Passion itself gives us the colours, the canvas, the plan, but the picture for individuals has to be worked out in themselves. Each person has a theological duty through baptism to discover what the open-lidded treasure chest of the Passion contains for them to display to the world. That display is of the nature of sanctity.

We are here to continue and 'make complete' that salvation story. The parables give us hints and clues of the nature of that salvation and show us the mind of the master who guides our brush and pen. The open-endedness of the Passion enables each age and each person within that age to fit the needs and culture of their generation to the salvation story. The Passion is a master key unlocking grace for each and every century.

Lastly the sea-shore. There can be nothing as real as crucifixion, but nothing as mysterious as the narrative of the Passion. The whole narrative from the entry into Jerusalem until the far side of the tomb breathes both an ordinariness, at times, as well as the inexplicable. In fact, as so many of the parables display, the effect is achieved by the juxtaposition of both reality and mystery, and their merger. We stand on the sea-shore between the reality of God's love and the mystery of his total absence, between the apparent upholding of the Father and the depth of his desertion of the Son. Between moments of confidence in the early days of Passion week and the complete despair of Calvary. Between the knowledge of God's love shining through in so much of the Gospel, and the terrifying blackness on the Cross that God's love is gone and perhaps was never there. That is the plumbing of the reality of the depths that God and his Son are prepared to undergo. And no theology of the atonement can cope with it, thank goodness. Rattle substitution theories and the rest about as much as you like. Nothing satisfies, because we can do no other but stand on that shore in wonder.

So I ask you this Lent to ask yourself not so much what can I do in terms of discipline or even discipleship, but to hunt, to research, to explore the nature of God as seen in his Son, using the parables as compass and guide in that exploration. Daring too, as our Lord does, to risk all the easy answers that so much of theology has given us down the ages, and which the Church still does so often. Daring to have no answers at all yet still carrying on to the end. In other words joining our Lord as far as we can in his work of exploration of every agony of humanity. Through the ordinary parables explore the parable of Christ's Passion and through the parable of his Passion explore the nature of humanity.

2

The Unjust Steward

St Luke 16: 1–13

It was a dangerous job being a medieval jester. Employed by a lord to entertain, to make a fool of oneself, to perform acrobatics on the table. At times to take minds off the food in the same way as spices did, and lead the household with merriment into drunkenness. But like all jesters and most good comedians there was a serious side to the job. They were there to crack the sort of joke that got under the skin, between the joints of the harness and beneath the armour of the lord. Prick his conscience by means of a witticism. Bring to him things of the community that needed a look at by use of a joke, a jest. Draw attention to faults or even immoralities inside the household by means of a story, in much the same way as Nathan the prophet did to David about Uriah the Hittite. The jester watched the lord and his community and turned what he saw into a knife-edged wisecrack. A very costly business at times. Even more risky since he was powerless. He saw into people's minds and souls and produced his daggers of jesting and did it at the risk to his job and comfort.

All done from a position of weakness. Perhaps all good comedy always has that otherness to it, whether it be exposing community or individual wrongs and prides or whether it be close to tragedy. Many comedians have always had a note of tragedy within them. Powerful, though with the power hidden within the velvet glove of humour. People will take almost anything when it is wrapped in laughter.

There is no suitable definition of a parable, but our Lord's are often the sayings, stories and swords of a very skilful jester. He is an expert script-writer of conscience-pricking comedy. There are many designed to strike at the hearts and minds of the rulers of the day. Plenty that draw attention to the blindness of orthodoxy, the deafness of authority. He is the ultimate Jewish jester, using exaggeration, pathos, surprise and verbal colour to poke under the ephod, take a swipe at the phylacteries and mock the riches of those in power. I suspect in this parable there is a hidden mocking of some local scenario which was known to the first hearers but is lost to us. No wonder there were times in his ministry when the crowds began by marvelling at his wit and wisdom but ended by trying to lynch him. Likewise the rulers, though done in a more careful and planned way.

Jest and comedy may come from a position of powerlessness as it did with Jesus. As has been often said, Jesus had no diploma from Jerusalem, no official status, though his followers called him Rabbi or teacher, and he probably had a Galilean accent which perhaps didn't give him points with officialdom. Lord Reith would not have had him on the BBC. But comedy with a serious twist, with a sting in the tail of conscience, also renders the target powerless too, very often. It is impossible to answer back to the truth of jest except with jest. And the witty phrase is what the people would have taken home and rolled round their minds. They would have shared it with those they met. 'Have you heard this one?' The power of cartoon that renders the powerful powerless is more infuriating and infectious than other forms of verbal arrows. Used in abundance and often unscrupulously by the modern media and the press in particular.

As I said, a lot of the Gospel narrative probably contains hidden references that are also hidden to us. Contemporary events that were local and had only just happened were used by Jesus to catch the crowds and penetrate the authorities. Maybe the purpose of this particular parable is completely lost, which is why we find it an almost impossible story to understand. Why also St Luke, a Greek coming to it from outside, felt compelled to add some spare maxims which don't help its interpretation. Perhaps Luke didn't know what it meant either!

Let me develop jest and comedy as the art of the powerless, the only weapon at times of the weak, the napalm of the religious terrorist, a bit further. If it is to be of influence, to get under the skin, it has first of all to reach its target, but not destroy that target. Yes, it infuriated the crowds at times and often the scribes and Pharisees, but it was so carefully done that although it stuck it wasn't so outrageous in its attack that it could be disregarded and discarded. It often has to hurt, too, but not so much that it made healing impossible. As far as we can see, Jesus had that art perfectly shaped and used it with consummate skill.

Secondly it had to be also something that grasped the attention of both the crowds and the religious rulers. Pointed jest that leaves one group cold usually both fails and annoys. Christ had the amazing art of selecting subjects that involved and penetrated all groups within his audience in one way or another. 'And here's one for the Sadducees' won't do, unless others understand as well.

Thirdly, and very obviously, it must contain something that can touch the hearts and minds of the vast majority of hearers and lead to thought and, he hoped, change. That is the only method the powerless possess with which to do their work. Such were Christ's parables, though as I have suggested a lot of the local colour and much of the local humour cannot be recaptured.

One other point before I say something about the jester and the Cross. Not only did those jesters, those story-tellers of old, often have to wrap up their meaning in humour, the best of them used language which through the nature of its rhythms and cadences seared itself into mind and memory and enabled the listeners, like cows, to take the food away with them for further chewing later. And it goes even further than that with the supreme story-teller, the supreme jester, our Lord, even in translation. His cadences, his rhythms, the beauty of his language are at times as important, if not more so, than the immediate meaning of the story. The music of the language is as much an element of change and 'conversion' as the meaning of the story itself. He knew that if you overloaded stories with meaning (turning them into allegories, for instance) at the expense of linguistic poetry, a shifty sort of moralizing crept in and accessibility departed. How I wish modern liturgists, to go down a side-road, would remember that. They have tended to push too much meaning, too much theology into a collect or a liturgical prayer, at the expense of rhythm and beauty, and it becomes a sermon. I say to myself, 'There goes the liturgist again, never losing an opportunity to preach at me'.

But a function of liturgy, as with parable, is not only for the words to have meaning but to wrap that meaning in phrases of beauty so that they transport as well as give rise to thought. It was essential that we had alternatives to the old liturgies such as the Book of Common Prayer, in which some of those services entered into mind and memory with ease and took you without hype to the presence of God.

Meaningful they might be, but they took you to another country by their rhythms, beauty and natural familiarity – not with the unreality that some Christian mantras can have but with the reality of artistry. St John of the Cross talks of such liturgical and prayerful beauty. In prayer, he says, it is as if we are trying to cross a divide, a yard, a street which is between God's land and ours. The yard is guarded by a dog. Some prayers and liturgies can act as a bone which keeps the dog quiet and busy while your spirit crosses over. The bone doesn't lose its reality (the bone is meaningful!), but it also enables us to fly. Cathedral Choral Evensong can do much the same thing, and despite our transport during it to that 'land of pure delight' we are still fully involved in the worship. Liturgists need to understand that we don't have to participate verbally in the worship all the time to be involved both in it and with God at the same time.

And all that because I think parables and sometimes their associated maxims not only have a message and meaning, usually one to work out for yourself, but also a meaning made real by the glorious rhythm of the words. They can transport you to the presence of Christ, which makes it more likely that the meaning goes home. The 'liturgy' of the parable can gear you for performance. Jesus may be the stimulator of our minds and muscles by his parables, but he is also the musician of our souls.

And now, a few words about the Cross and the jester, for the Cross and Passion are the jester's scene. There is the mocking of Jesus by the soldiers, by the crowds and by the Jewish leaders. Mocking which is the jester's work now turned on the divine jester. But what the crowd and leaders say in their mocking of Christ as king, their mocking of Christ as saviour is, unknown to them in their blindness, the truth. All is emphasized by the sceptre which was the wand the medieval jester carried and all is pictured by the purple robe of imperial power. The 'acrobatics' of crucifixion, the twisting of the jester's body is a witness to the fact that the Cross turns value after value in the world's thinking upside down. As the hymn states, this is the Saviour's dancing day. The word 'jest' has the same root as that of the word 'gesture', a performance, in its original meaning. This performance is God's final gesture in the salvation of his creation. It is the divine comedy which undermines the positions of power just as the jester did. I'm not sure that I could justify it theologically, but I have a feeling that it is only the powerless who can bring salvation to all those above them in the pack. The powerful cannot bring salvation to those less strong than themselves. Such is the crucified jester. He is at the nadir of weakness and is hence able to bring salvation to all.

The Parable

The parable of the Unjust Steward itself has a wonderful compactness about it. Not a word wasted. For me it certainly has the stamp of Jesus on it, in the masterly use of phrase, and in the brilliance of scene description. It has all the marks of the maestro of story-telling. So much an accomplished artist that he needs no long setting of the scenery. You are there, part of the setting in a few words. There is no 'once upon a time' vocabulary. Straight in. If this is so I tend to think that this is a reworking of a local tale, a recent scandal, which his hearers would have been familiar with. It was humming on the local bush telegraph and no lead-up was necessary. It was a case of – as you have undoubtedly seen in this morning's newspaper. I suspect, too (pure conjecture), that those parts of the story that the people already knew were only hinted at and have been lost. St Luke retells a later version circulating in the Church and attached three or four proverbs to it. Certainly, scholars find several inconsistencies in it. Language and syntax that don't tie up. It's Mozart with touches of pure genius, but with some of the sonata form and the notes tampered with by later editors.

But there is a wonderful audacity, too, about the parable, which shouts that the words are those of Jesus. We presume that, like the rich man, our Lord commends not what the steward actually did but the reasons why he did it. When a crisis arises you take immediate action and astute action to save your skin. Jesus and the early Church were convinced that the last times were upon us, so immediate resolute action was necessary. Or, as the second little proverb seems to be saying, use the worldly to ensure your place in the heavenly. Or, as the Collect from the Book of Common Prayer puts it, 'We may so pass through things temporal that we finally lose not the things eternal.'

The third and to some extent the fourth maxims are for me almost impossible to interpret and I suggest we must be careful not to force Jesus's mind into phrases that probably do not contain his thinking at all. Or, if they do, the context has been lost. Let me use a historical illustration which descends to nonsense in much the same way.

When in the sixteenth century dissection of the human body started again they found certain structures that didn't tie up with Aristotelian anatomy. But Aristotle was infallible. Therefore some of the men of that day assumed that the human body had changed since Aristotle's day.

In the same way, St Luke gives us the words of the parable and the proverbs as if these were the actual words of Jesus. Do we have to twist our thinking, as those anatomists did, and believe the story in exactly the way it is recorded by the evangelist, as the infallible words of Christ? The excitement, it seems to me, is not to look at the morality within the parable and the oddities within the proverbs attached, but to find the character of Jesus hidden within the passage despite the passage itself. Jesus is teasing the crowd with a story the context of which is lost to us. Perhaps teasing *us* even more. Audaciouly using a rogue to point out the urgency of our condition and the need for immediate action. We have here the supreme jester, telling a jokey story which also tells us the sort of man he was. And it is his incredible skill at creating atmosphere which we can still feel. The crowds waiting on his words. His skill at presenting a story which leaves you with a knowing, but not with a worked-out meaning, as well as with a greater understanding of Christ's divine insight, even if you couldn't put an understanding of that insight into careful prose. My father used to have jokes which we laughed at uproariously, but we weren't quite certain why. They said more about him and his quiet profundity than they did about the nature of the joke. Faith is partly about that 'meaningless' understanding which we grasp by just reading the Gospels.

That inexpressible knowing is also how we should view the Cross as well as the ordinary theology and understanding of it. Such knowing has converting and changing power by its very presence, a presence that needs no description. The line from 'Abide with me', 'Hold thou thy Cross before my closing eyes' has that sort of feel about it. We need the scholars who can penetrate with exciting depth. We need the mystics who give us words that 'music' their way into our souls. But we also need stories and symbols, parables, which tease their way into our being almost without our knowing they are doing so. God's unspoken foolishness of which the Cross is the supreme example has that power.

3

The Rich Man and Lazarus

St Luke 16: 19–31

I'm bound to admit that I have difficulties about automatic pie in the sky for those who were short of pie on earth. Equal difficulties, too, about eternal denial of treats for those who feasted on earth below. That is clearly not the central theme of this parable which is a reworking of a tale, possibly from Egypt, which was doing the rounds at the time. All preachers pinch other people's stories and remodel them to their needs and our Lord seems to have been a master at the art.

But pie rewards and the lack of them gives me a chance to throw out a few questions about justice, retribution and punishment, about sin and responsibility and so on, which I touch on in another chapter. Do our Christian concepts concerning all of these and many of the concepts and dicta in the Bible really correspond with the mind of God as seen in the sacrificial life and atoning death of his Son, let alone our secular concepts and the way we deal with offenders? This section of the chapter must be viewed only as questions, which I hope could be thrown about in many types of discussion group. They are subjects which it is impossible to come to with an open mind. We are influenced by our backgrounds and culture, by the way we have contacted law and order, and those we have known concerned with it. But they are subjects and questions that are almost top of the Christian list for thought and action in a world where revenge and retribution are the stock-in-trade of individuals and nations.

At the beginning of this story, filched by our Lord, it is clear that Lazarus (which means 'God helps') got a large helping after death while the rich man was tormented. The beginning of the ancient story (told perhaps by our Lord with his tongue in his cheek) appears to assume that this is what will happen, and most of us assume it is a picture of reality. So the first question to ask is: is there too much clarity about such things both in the Bible and in some theological and popular thinking? Are there too many phrases, bordering on clichés, that are accepted as correct?

We assume that a common cliché such as 'the punishment ought to fit the crime' is sensible and proper. We assume that punishment is a right response to crime or misdemeanour in families or in individuals. We assume that when a judge gives a harsh sentence to someone for a particular crime, because he wants to send out a signal (another cliché) to other offenders, that is a fair and even a Christian thing to do. And, more theologically, we assume that the saying 'God hates the sin and loves the sinner, and we should do the same', is again a Christian way of thinking. I have my doubts that our doings and our personalities can be so glibly separated. Clichés and accepted clarity about sin and responsibility, that the beginning of this parable illustrates, most of the time probably prevent us thinking in a Christlike way. We say to ourselves 'That seems sensible to me' and we do not think twice about it. I am of course glad that Lazarus was happy and comfortable in Abraham's bosom after all he went through on earth, but the rich man's parched torment is another matter and needs a second or third thought about its appropriateness. So my first thought is to beware, a lot of the time, of over-crisp thinking, even biblically crisp thinking. It can often be a disguise for something nasty.

Secondly, is the theory which prescribes heaven for some and hell for others, together with much of our criminal and legal system, really a refined version of an eye for an eye and a tooth for a tooth? Do we expect or even require God to award punishments after death, because we think a sinner must pay his due, and if he hasn't done so on earth he must have an eye removed in the afterlife? Certainly the Old Testament and some of the New are full of such, and our theological and legal thinking make it clear that wrongdoing must be paid for, though the legal system never for one moment thinks that righteousness should be rewarded. It is its own reward, we are glibly told.

In this parable, insensitive luxury-living had to be paid for. The punishment must fit the crime. Wine for Dives on earth, therefore not a drop of liquid in Hades. Is most of our thinking on these issues a heavily disguised (and in the press a not so heavily disguised) form of revenge? We cannot bear for one moment that anyone should 'get away with it', and if someone doesn't get punished in this life then punished they must be, we assume, in the afterlife. I desperately hope that the innocent sufferers, the starving, the afflicted, will in some way be compensated, but that is a very far cry from our desire that the wicked should suffer according to their deserts.

A very famous and rather tender-hearted medieval theologian states that part of the joy of heaven is seeing the wicked suffering in hell. He was not, I suspect, being cruel but saying that wickedness must be seen to be destroyed. But how does all that tie up with our Lord's suffering for the guilty as well as for the innocent? What does atonement mean as far as the Stalins and Hitlers of this world are concerned? Does it mean that the sin is atoned for but not the repentant or unrepentant sinner? I offer no answers, just throw it into the pool. In other words, can complete justice and complete love be peaceful bedfellows?

Thirdly, the more you go down the path of concentrating on sin and evil the more it implies that sin is more important and more powerful than goodness, and that evil is more overwhelming than love. It is said that when the first death warrant for the execution of a soldier was put in front of Queen Victoria for signature she asked if there were anything good to be said about him. 'He is kind and gentle to his wife,' said the secretary. 'That is enough', said the Queen, and refused to sign the warrant. The *a fortiori* argument again applies here. If a mere monarch can count gentleness as a cause for reprieve, how much more shall the King of Heaven reprieve his children who offend.

Fourthly, we have to realize that morality is a shifting sand, not only in its grades of seriousness, but whether a deed be sinful or not. As circumstances change so does morality. Clearly there are some simple moral rules such as, never be cruel in any way. You have to be cruel to be kind doesn't, I hope, mean anything of the sort. Clearly we must take responsibility for our sins, unless there are medical reasons for not doing so, and take some responsibility for the sins of the society we live in. But the overwhelming Gospel, Good News, is that Christ also takes responsibility for our sins, and is able to turn them into aspects of love. His love also follows us around whatever state of sinfulness we are in. God is close to us whatever we are doing, whatever we are up to. God is involved with us, tending us, both in our goodness and in our wickedness and that is true perhaps even the other side of death. He is silently beseeching us wherever, whatever, whenever. So there are a few difficulties to consider without set minds and without hard-line clarity and perhaps without hard-line charity as well.

The Parable

I find the parable of Lazarus and the Rich Man enchanting as a tale. It is a great story. I wonder if our Lord may have had his tongue in his cheek as he told it. One of the original stories on which it may have been based is that of a poor scholar compared, in the same way as Lazarus and Dives, with a rich publican who feasted every day, was robed in purple wool and had Egyptian cotton underwear. Their fates in the afterlife were the same as the characters in the parable.

The description of Lazarus and his poverty is a masterly picture of a beggar, probably a cripple, thrown down on his pitch outside the gates of the rich man's house. He would have been glad to have fed himself with the cleaning-up scraps of bread left by Dives and his guests at the table. You can almost see them scraping round the plates with them and then throwing them away. We get a picture of the wild dogs of the streets pushing their noses into the beggar to see if he were ready for eating yet. Jesus creates the scene for his hearers with consummate skill. They would have seen similar sights many times, and would probably have been familiar with the original version of the tale. They would certainly have been familiar with the teaching behind the first part of it.

This is the only parable where a character has a name: Lazarus – God helps. It may be that he is named because the Jewish version of the story contained it, or because God was going to help him in the afterlife. Or could it be because the crowds also knew the story of Jesus raising the brother of Mary and Martha from the dead? That may be impossible because of timing, but the name is significant from every angle.

But the feature I find fascinating, as in so many parables, is the brilliant way in which Jesus takes them from the familiar to the surprising. There he is on familiar ground, a well-known story, about role reversal in the life after death, all common territory for his hearers, and all done as usual with a mixture of pathos and humour. Then suddenly they are in another theological world. We find that the parable is not really about Lazarus and the Rich Man but about the six brothers. Time and time again in the parables Jesus begins with the familiar, gets them on his side by repeating a well-known story or common occurrence in a compelling way, and then with a swift stroke of the verbal pen he is introducing a completely different, challenging theological theme. Not beginning where they are in a patronizing way, but leading them by tempting morsels into the banquet of strange but needful fodder. He does it with the Unjust Judge, the Cheating Steward, and with the Good Samaritan, with the Pearl of Great Price, and here he is at it again. A parable version of one or two of Haydn's symphonies, 'The Surprise', for instance.

The theological message here is clear. 'If they hear not Moses and the prophets neither will they repent though one rose from the dead.' It is almost the central message of all departments of life. If we learn nothing from political prophets, and even less from religious ones; if we learn nothing from God's nudges of old, and even less than nothing from his present-day nudges, however dramatic, then we will learn nothing from resuscitation (Lazarus) or from resurrection. And depending on parentage counts for nothing either, even though they be Abraham's children, just as our Church parentage counts for nothing if we continue in our blindness and stubbornness. As far as the religious leaders of Jesus's day were concerned this was unforgivable fighting talk.

The demanding of a sign has always been a sign of impenitence, says our Lord. We seldom change our ways however, even if we are given one. But I find the reverse equally difficult: those people who see certain events that gobble up innocent and guilty alike as being sent by God. An American Baptist pastor announced, as have many other extreme Christians, that AIDS was sent as a punishing sign from God. When challenged with the fact that many innocent people have died from AIDS through blood tranfusion and rape, he replied that the innocent have to suffer with the guilty. That may indeed be so, but to apply it directly to God's action borders on the obscene.

Signs can also be mere superstition, which Plutarch defines as to be in ignorant dread of God's divine power, without any joy in his goodness. We dread something which is about to afflict us and hope that God will give us a sign of its outcome or protect us if we perform certain acts (entrails of a chicken in ancient Rome), and when they do or don't happen the dread increases. Jesus's sayings about signs and their offspring are some of his fiercest, because they destroy people's souls. 'Truly no sign will be given to this generation.'

So where does all this leave us? Neither dread of Hades, nor dramatic signs, nor miracles, not even rising from the dead, resurrection, have the power to change the hearts of sinful humanity, says our Lord. Not even his own resurrection. Is there nothing that can appeal to humanity's soul, both individually and corporately? Is there nothing that can break through the layer of insensitivity? Signs only speak to us of the possible presence and power of a hidden divinity. Hell only speaks to us of a divinity who has the power finally to reject those he is said to love. In the Old Testament we read of a God whose power, it seems, produces mayhem in Egypt on innocent and guilty and produces fire and earthquakes to frighten men's souls in the wilderness. Such happenings may terrify or produce awe and wonder, but they do not touch the heart or persuade the mind. Even our Lord's resurrection is a confirmation of God's power over death, manifested to men and women whose hearts have already been changed, and not a public, dramatic event to force a change on unbelieving hearts. Resurrection may be the foundation of the Christian faith, but has it no power to convince the stubborn or change the will? Likewise Marley's ghost: a result of indigestion, Scrooge decided, and did nothing to alter his personality. Force of any kind, it would seem, cannot change hearts freely and permanently.

In the end, is the only possibility for breakthrough the Cross and Passion? That was the question Jesus asked himself and his Father in the Garden of Gethsemane, and the answer was a terrifying knowledge that it was so. For the signs I have spoken of (the resurrection apart) have no reality of tenderness. They do not manifest the ultimate of God's flesh-and-blood love. It is only silent, innocent suffering that can shout the nature of God. The rich man's five brothers would have been immune to the reappearance of Lazarus, Jesus tells us in the parable. Could they have resisted so completely the power of tenderness seen in Christ's Cross?

So where does all that leave us? For modern men and women, the fear of hell, the manifestation of signs and miracles, even the resurrection itself, may be acknowledged as a possible revealing of the presence of a hidden divinity, but no more, and I probably count myself in that bunch of waverers. In the end, to add a personal coda to this chapter, all I want to see and know is the nature of God's love, and I do not see that ultimate love in those dramatic signs.

Yes, I may hope for resurrection. I may hope for the joys of the Kingdom of Heaven. I may hope for the sight of the Holy Trinity, unbearable though that may be. But it is the nature of the Godhead as seen in the Cross and Passion that suffices. We cannot ask for more. It is the signature of the divine writer on human hearts.

4

The Sower

St Mark 4: 1–20

One of my delights with a confirmation class and within my teaching career was to see the excitement on the faces of eleven-year-olds when fascinated by the synoptic problem. Doing detective work on how and why the first three Gospels differ in their description of the same event. Why there is material in one of them that isn't in the other. Why one Gospel has more detail about an event and a miracle. Why there are two donkeys in Matthew's description of Palm Sunday for instance, while Mark and Luke have only one beast. Why we think St Mark is the earliest Gospel. What embellishments and changes have been popped in by the early Church. All immensely exciting for young minds and for them confirms both the normality and the extraordinary nature of Holy Writ. And one of the richest mines of such thrills is the parables.

Trying to compare similar ones in different Gospels. Trying to dissect probable additions or twists. Sorting out the motives behind those differences. Sherlock Holmes has nothing on the good, young synoptic hunter. Not only does this stimulate minds, it gives Scripture a reality and an honesty that swallowing it all, hook, line and sinker, never achieves. It has a beauty and a risk and a wonderful open-endedness. I have met many a young potential theologian in such groups. How many Thomas Aquinases have we missed out on by serving up take-it-or-leave-it courses? Why do I find it so seldom happens in Lent Bible Studies for adults? Why do I rarely find it in courses constructed for those who are new to the faith or finding out about the roots of it all? There is not much point in having faith in the Bible, or even studying it, unless you know first of all the nature of its trustworthiness.

The parable of the Sower and its explanation in Matthew 13, and even more so that of the Wheat and Darnel in the same chapter, is a good place to start such investigations perhaps, to start the hunt for the reason why; to start the biggest excitement of all in discovering the Lord of Scripture. Any group would surely be better for joining that chase.

Again, why are teachers and clergy often so reticent, so unwilling, to do this detective work with their people? Do we not trust them? Do we think they are not capable of understanding it? Do we think it will destroy their faith and it is too risky a venture? Which leads me to a few other points in this introduction before I say something about the parable itself.

I have spoken already about one type of meaning when talking about the parable of the Unjust Steward. But there is also another tyranny of meaning. The desire to have a 'this is what it means and that's that' approach to Scripture. The tyranny of certitude. Maybe this is not what the early Church was doing when it popped in the explanation of the parable of the Sower, but that is what it has become. 'This is what the parable means and that is that.' Certainly the first few centuries of the Church loved allegory and typology. It enabled them to deal with lots of the unpleasant bits of Scripture. St Augustine a few centuries later constructed his allegories of the parables not to encase their meaning, I hope, but as a sort of complex meditational game.

Living dangerously is surely better than living in chains. Even putting a basic tenet of the faith up for debate now and again may be risky, but the gains are usually more than the losses. Creeds and basic biblical beliefs are, after all, only pictures and parables of the Almighty. Although our Lord's pictures and insights into the nature of his Father are for the Christian the nearest that humanity can conceive. What in the end that reality is, is the final partaking of glory. All of which has been said a hundred times, but Lent is a good time to remind ourselves of our limitations and that goes for individuals, the Church and Scripture. Yes, I would consider that even the Bible is a book of divine inspiration and human limitation.

Much of what I have said is about control. The faith-police have dictated to us over the centuries and sometimes they have worn monastic habits, and sometimes they have worn mitres or Protestant clothing. Doctrines that require to be defended by doing ghastly things to those who have hesitations about those doctrines don't increase my faith in the validity of those doctrines. If the Church authorities (whoever they are) can't convince by gentle reason, by loving conviction, by biblical and credal excitement, there must be something suspicious about their starting-points.

One last point, rather nearer the parables than what I have just said, even if tangentially so. A feature I find enormously attractive about them is their integration of the secular and the sacred. Again, it is mostly a feeling, but you shiver with the sensation of the holy as Jesus tells the story and reflects the light off the diamond of description. His starting phrase, 'The Kingdom of Heaven is like this', and somehow or other it permeates the whole parable. It's not the Sunday School definition of an earthly story with a heavenly meaning. The whole story takes on the divine, the heavenly. It is as if Jesus with his complete realization that the world is God's creation puts that realization into the tale itself. The parable of the Sower possesses the Lord of creation in the most exhilarating way. In fact, whenever Jesus or holy people talk about the ordinary, you feel they are talking about God, and you find that grasping of the ordinary by divinity in people of every walk of life and in those of other faiths as well. This cocktail of the ordinary and the holy is not the sole possession of Christians, as we all know. Such people are living parables and their silent, beautiful, open-ended expression of this sanctifies the ordinary and normalizes the sacred. Puts it within our reach. The parables of Jesus are a parable of his divine and human nature.

The Parable

The parable of the Sower is often used as the standard example of a parable. It is only so without the explanation, without what many people find a rather tedious allegory of it all. It must have been an early addition, as it is there in Mark, the earliest Gospel, with Matthew and Luke copying from Mark almost word for word. The earliness of it gives it a fascination despite all that I have said. It is unlikely to have been by Mark as it not his style at all.

Chop off the explanation and you have a story of wonderful brevity and one which grips the imagination at once. You can see it all. As soon as you realize that in Palestine at that time ploughing took place after the seed was sown and not before it, it again makes the picture clearer and reasonable. Thorns and weeds would have grown up during the resting season. Villagers would have trampled a footpath through the field as villagers do in empty fields today. What looked like careless sowing on the paths at once becomes understandable. Some of the soil would have been very shallow and rocky, some deep and fertile. Maybe it was an immediate parable, as Jesus looked up and saw the sower throwing his seed around as the villagers walked along the beaten track. He saw the weeds already there, and knew the shallow and rocky soil of his native land. It was all a home video for him.

But as Jesus sees the sower he remembers the harvest to come. He remembers the yearly miracle, and all the difficulties and all the failures are forgotten in the vision of the fields white for harvest. As he does so frequently, Jesus is describing the coming of the Kingdom of God in terms of harvest. And what a harvest it is. A superabundant reaping despite some wretched beginnings. (It may be a harvest of the Word of God but Jesus is unlikely to have identified such in the parable. It is not a phrase that he uses.) It is our Lord at his most confident, and his hearers would have taken it away and thought about it personally perhaps, but just as likely in terms of the community of Israel. It is our Lord thinking that all things are possible. The people will listen, they will respond. Their hearts will be turned. No wonder the Church felt it had to separate the parable and its explanation with a section that makes it clear that despite looking, the people will never see, despite listening, they will never understand.

The writers, whoever they were, knew that our Lord's confidence in his message and in his hearers hadn't been borne out. Isaiah had to come to the rescue to explain the failure. All very sad, because whatever the parables were they were not tales to baffle the hearers. They were not stories to prevent understanding. On the contrary, they were there to excite minds, to have a clarity of expression, if not necessarily of meaning. They were there to open up new ways and areas of an understanding of the nature of God, not to diddle them. Nor were they stories for the elite, just for the inner circle of disciples, whom Jesus found just as stupid as the rest. Our Lord was desperate at this stage that everybody should hear the good news of the Kingdom of God. His was an 'open secret'.

So in this parable we have peasant beauty and an open-endedness; open to the world and open to the Gospel in joyful simplicity and expectation. It is the story of a laughing young man who adores those he is speaking to and knows he has the power to captivate them. But by the time of the sacrificial Passover in John 12 the seed is no longer the straightforward bearer of the harvest. It must first die, and only if it dies does it bear a rich harvest. Death and sacrifice are now at the heart of a harvest from the Gospel. If the seed doesn't die it remains a seed and nothing more. Without the shedding of blood there is no harvest, no Gospel. Death is a condition for harvest.

Here is the high priest of the Gospel who is himself the seed of that Gospel and the death that attains it. Some Christians are frightened, and at times rightly so, in tying up death, sacrifice and the new life of the new covenant. The sacramental harvest. But that sacramental parable of death is the starting-point of the actual Passion and it is only by our personal and community involvement in it that we can be led to a personal and communal resurrection harvest. It is worth a Lenten meditation and discussion about how all these things are tied up and how they should be shown forth in the life of the Church.

One last thought. St Paul uses almost exactly similar language in 1 Corinthians 15 when talking of resurrection, our personal harvest. He points out that what is inside the seed that dies governs the personal resurrection that follows. Not a comfortable thought on one level, but the most comforting of all on another.

So in this saddest of all the parables the beautiful, confident, happy Lord looks forward to a preaching harvest, to a listening people, to an accepted ministry, as he scatters the seeds of the Gospel. Later, however, though unknown to him at this stage, it must be the seed that dies if there is to be any harvest at all. And sowing that seed is the job of the Church which is his body, and that is the reason for its involvement in the state and in the world.

5

The Unmerciful Servant

St Matthew 18: 23–35

It is important for us to realize again and again that in human terms the Gospel is mad. Sheer folly, as St Paul calls it, from beginning to end. We have become so adjusted to it that we take all the craziness for granted. Impossible that the creator of the universe and every other universe should appear in the form of helplessness. Taking his stand on a preaching 'platform', often the sea-shore; talking about not striking back, however much provoked, and claiming fanciful things such as poverty as a happier state than riches and that the meek are the inheritors of the earth. In human terms patently not true. Few believed him then and few have believed him since. And perhaps the parables are the most foolish set of stories of all. The Vineyard in Mark 12 is plain crazy. The one I am about to write about – forgiveness – is a sort of forgiveness that sensible Christians wouldn't countenance. Forgiveness beyond thinking, unconditional, with nothing to pay, no repentance required. Then there is the parable of equal pay packets for all, even for those that have worked for little more than five minutes. Then one about a master applauding a cheating Steward. The Prodigal Son too – at least a couple of theological corkscrews there. They may only be colourful tales to light up an aspect of God's nature. Over-the-top tales. The Kingdom of Heaven is like this. But destroy the ethos of those parables, and you are back to some of the fiercer bits of St Paul and much of the way to how the Church has behaved down the ages. You are back to the death of the butterfly of the Gospels and its pinning out on the display board, totally immovable.

And all that foolishness leads up to what St Paul claims with passion to the point of tears is the greatest foolishness of all. The parable

of Christ's crucifixion, death and resurrection. How could a criminal's death be the crowning glory, the sin-atoning purpose and
plan of God Almighty? And if that is so, God must take the
responsibility for, and be the architect of that painful piece of
lunacy. In other words, we have a God who through his Son's life
and death turns the normal, sensible, obvious standards and thinking of this world upside down. A crucifixion, if Mark is to be
believed, where all the things that humankind depends on disappear. Adding folly to folly. The story is total blackness. Jesus dies in
total despair, with the conviction that God has deserted him
utterly. Jesus who was convinced throughout his ministry that his
Father was close beside him, that he was showing forth in deed
and word the nature of his Father, now finds his Father has
departed into the blackness when his support was most needed.
Put like that it sounds a black farce. What sort of God have we
here?

I would claim that that is what this parable of forgiveness is about,
extrapolated as it must be if its exaggeration is to make sense. Because
that death of Christ is about total, redeeming forgiveness. Redemption at an unbelievable cost, as in the parable. And that is what God's
involvement in the Cross in about too. A God who allows his precious Son, his only child, put in human terms, to plumb the utter
depths of despair, desertion, hopelessness, blackness and failure, so that
humanity in all its awfulness can be redeemed. Individual, personal
religion is only part of this redemption, it is a corporate affair as well,
as we will see in the parable. In his lifetime and in his death Christ
covers the full range of human emotions that humanity feels and
suffers, and all types of people are involved in the drama, so that all
can be forgiven and redeemed. And I need hardly say that God the
Father, if he is God, and God the Holy Spirit, if he is the all-pervading
Spirit, are there too in the total darkness agonizing with the Son,
though unseen, unheard, and unfelt through necessity. Such I hope is
our creed. God the Holy Trinity shares the dreadful lunacy of the
Cross in full measure, so that our appalling values, our sensible values,
are turned upside down and which crucified love proclaims is the
right way up.

The theme of this chapter is unconditional forgiveness. We try in
our folly (though folly requires it) to construct little schemes to
explain all this beyond-our-understanding forgiveness which once
more through the Cross reunites heaven and earth. What we call

the atonement. We even give theories of the atonement pompous little titles. Perhaps, but only perhaps, God's love and justice, humanity's sin and the beyond-our-understanding forgiveness of God, our wickedness and its cost to God in redemption, all need squaring. But the substitution theory of the atonement and other attempts to explain it seem to me rather horrid, and sometimes appallingly nasty attempts to satisfy a wrathful God. But what does satisfying a wrathful God mean? That our sins mount up in an Augean stable which has to be washed out with the blood of our Herculean Lord? Simplistic though it may seem, I am happy to rest content in the skill of God's love. In the all-embracing artistry of his mercy as seen in the extremity of the Cross and in the extreme cost to the Lord this parable speaks about. There is that wonderful stanza from a poem by Auden,

> You need not see what someone is doing.
> To know if it is his vocation.
> You have only to watch his eyes; a cook mixing a sauce,
> A surgeon making a primary incision,
> A clerk completing a bill of lading,
> Wear the same rapt expression
> Forgetting themselves in function.

God on the Cross is that skill of love, he is lost in the function of mercy. The skill and function of such love is beyond our understanding and that love is the only answer. Generously mad in its outpouring, as the parable shows. Crazily glorious in its swamping of our sins. I ask no more than that.

The Parable

An amazing parable that gets its effect by laughable exaggeration and contrast. The Jews, it seems, loved hyperbole and would have found it enormously amusing. That's if it were told publically rather than just to the disciples, until they realized that it ended in a personal arrow or two. It is planks and motes transferred onto the field of forgiveness. Our Lord attempting to open a few national, theological, personal eyes, minds and hearts in a land where forgiveness was not at a premium. Rather like this country where we so often live in a revenge culture against certain types of offence, regardless of the age of the offender. Revenge stimulated and encouraged often by the media. As Martin Luther King used to say, 'If we go for the principle of an eye for an eye, a tooth for a tooth, we all end up blind and toothless.'

There is a beauty about the telling. Peter thinking that he is being very generous by offering to forgive his brother for an offence seven times, and Jesus stretching him to the elastic limit. So the introduction of the parable sets the scene. Peter expecting to be congratulated on his kindness.

Then comes the story, which is a wonderfully foolish one, for no one could have amounted a debt as large as that. Or if he had, it reflects on the stupidity of the king in allowing him to do so. And though I mustn't turn the parable into an allegory it moves me to think that in fact that is exactly what God does do to us. His generosity to our sinful spending knows no bounds. He gives us total freedom with our lives to over-spend sinfully as much as we care to. Here is a story where the artist paints the scene with the boldest of contrasting colours. Risk, too, was central to the story. Cancelling the debt without any conditions attached. No small print, but more about that later in this chapter. And I hope that the parable was open-ended as well. I find it very difficult to believe that the ending about delivering the unforgiving man to the torturers is dominical. Unless the torture is the disappointment and heartbreak of the king. Open-ended in that it is complete at verse 33. That is the spot where the sledge-hammer has struck between the eyes. Stopping there gives us a story of theological beauty, theological risk and theological open-endedness.

Let me concentrate on a couple of features that are completely obvious but probably central to the tale. First, once again, the amount. Clearly it is over the top. Nobody could mount up that amount. It is an impossibly crazy sum for a person to owe. It seems to me, however, that Christ goes through his life and particularly through the Passion using what people do and say to him, using his disciples' failure, using the whole trial and crucifixion drama as if he were collecting material for forgiveness. Every tiny detail is collected on to the rubbish cart for purification and atonement. Jesus is acting in the way the scapegoat does in the Book of Leviticus. And again, in that story it is the community's sins that are laden on to the goat's head who, like Christ, is sent out of the camp to death in the wilderness. Our Lord takes all those false relationships, all those betrayals, he takes hurts and hates, he takes accusations and bitterness, and takes them outside the camp for glorious changing.

For processing in fact. The Cross and resurrection change our sins into what God would have them be. The Greek word for sin, as preachers constantly tell us, really means an arrow which has fallen short of the mark. Christ's Cross picks up those arrows, processes them and takes them to the target where they are meant to be. He takes the lot, both our personal sins and those of the community of which we are a part. Hence the amount in the parable which represents all those appallingnesses of the past, the present and the future. All the horrors of history are also swept up into his nature and taken to that furnace of love. And he invites us to discharge all our emotions and fallings-short at him.

Perhaps you know the story of the man whose only daughter lay dangerously ill in hospital. Every day he visited her, calling in at the church on the way to pray before the crucifix there. After some time, her birthday arrived and he bought a beautiful cake, took it into the church on the way, and off he went to the hospital. When he arrived he found that his beloved daughter had just died. Anger, bitterness and misery overcame him and on his way back he went into the church and flung the cake at the crucifix. Christ takes all. Not just sanitized emotions and prayers, our respectable beseechings. The total amount. The parabolic pile. There are no limits. The national debt is cancelled out. The very fact that in the parable it is all expressed in terms of money says something of the cost, as St Paul likes to remind us. To use a purple passage, we are all winners in the remission lottery.

Secondly, let me concentrate on the unconditional nature of it all. The Lord in this crafted parable did not say, 'I will let you off on certain conditions'. The expectation that his wife and children would be sold, that he would be committed to slavery were not realized. Not even repentance was required. If there were sorrow it was the sorrow of the scared. No servitude, no repentance, no token repayment or what we call a penance were required. No punishment exacted. That is the picture of our Lord's forgiveness during his life and utterly so at his Passion. There are no conditions for forgiveness when it is given. That is what the Cross makes clear almost above all. 'Father, forgive them, they know not what they do.'

And there is no suggestion that the crucifiers were sorry in any way. Remission, forgiveness, is a treasure in store that we are cashing in on most of the time. And most of the time in our heart of hearts we think there should be some conditions. For others, anyway. After all, we argue, it is only fair that those who have wronged ought to show some form of remorse, pay for their sins in some way. But it is often forgiveness that produces the repentance, not the other way round, as we like to think.

Forgive one more story. A boy who came from a Christian home had offended his parents during Advent with a rather spectacular offence. He was asked to say sorry, but refused. And the more his parents gently asked, the more stubborn about it all he became. Christmas came nearer and nearer and as far as the boy was concerned he didn't care if his presents and rejoicings on Christmas Day were sacrificed, he was not going to say sorry. Eventually the great day arrived, and far from there being no gifts there were bigger and better ones than usual. His parents reckoned that the more wilful he had become the more the display of their love was required. Immediate collapse of wilfulness; tears of repentance flowed.

In most liturgies, after the confession the priest stands up and solemnly pronounces the absolution. It usually begins: Almighty God, who forgives all those who truly repent, etc. I find it hard to say, for although I believe that God loves us to be repentant, his absolution and forgiveness do not depend on it.

Alas, we do not believe that to be true, or that free forgiveness is either right or productive, so we hedge it round with every condition we can think of, and the bigger the offence the more conditions we make. And the tragedy is that because we do not believe that forgiveness is free for ourselves we cannot give it fully or freely to others. Often we find peanut wrongs harder to forgive than bigger ones, hence the last part of the parable.

One last thing, the parable makes clear that forgiveness is a gift and a very costly one. I enjoy hearing the prayer of consecration from the Book of Common Prayer which makes the cost absolutely clear by using the word 'remission'.

I have made it all sound banal and easy, I fear. In a sense it is easy for us, for all the work has been done by God in Christ. But in this parable and its spilling over into the Passion we are near the centre of the furnace of love radiating out from Holy Week and most of the time we are frightened to stand too close. Our personal sins are too precious to us and we cannot snatch the serpent off our shoulder.

Unconditional forgiveness is such a painful joy that we are often thankful there is darkness over the face of the land, so that we cannot see that it is being offered.

6

Jesus, the Good Shepherd

St John 10: 1–21

The headmaster of a famous school who had turned the use of mixed metaphors into an art form, once addressed his school with the words, 'If boys continue to skate on thin ice, they will find themselves in hot water'. The first eighteen verses of St John Chapter 10 are a metaphorical riot. If I compared parables with painters, sculptors and musicians, this is Picasso, Chagall, Henry Moore and Debussy all together. A riot of colour and imagination, something almost tangible but mysterious, and the sort of music that takes you places. Lots of 'I am' this or that, which have more than whispers of divinity about them. The phrase 'I am the good shepherd' could be a statement that transfers divinity to Jesus himself. The ever-present, the ever-'now' divinity, as at the burning bush in the wilderness. The cocktail of metaphors includes Jesus the door, a double door in fact, as well as the repeated good shepherd picture. A shepherd, too, with sheep in other folds, and a statement that all the sheep are eventually going to be one flock.

The beginning of the chapter is a wonderful hotchpotch of beautiful language and beautiful pictures. A risky business of protecting the sheep with his life, unlike the hired man. A shepherd who is totally free to lay down his life or not. And all this mixed up with some remarks about his Father who is in on the sacrifice too. It is open-ended, as well, in the sense that all the pictures, the allusions, whistle through the cine-projector without any explanation at all. Like so much of St John, it is left hanging in the air. What has been the subject of his meditations over the years. No wonder, if it were an actual situation, that the Jews found it all disturbing, more than bordering on the blasphemous and too much to take. In the same way as many of them found his remarks about eating his flesh and drinking his blood over the top. He is mad, why bother to listen to him? It is like the world's reaction to a number of scientists down the ages who have, like our Lord, spotted the master key to secret doors of the universe and no one has believed them, let alone joined them in going through those doors. They too have seen clues, as did Christ, to the nature of God through the nature of creation, but people have preferred the old ways of thinking.

Hidden in these shepherding words, however, are some difficulties. Watching shepherds is a fascinating business. Scottish ones in particular. Most of the time they appear to stand perfectly still, seemingly inattentive, leaning against a tree, perhaps. Just there. But every sheep is in within range of their watchful eye. He is always looking, noting, keeping a sharp eye open for dangers to the flock, for something not quite right with individual sheep. The watchfulness of the Scottish shepherd and perfectly of Jesus the good shepherd, is a picture of God's gift of freedom combined with his ever-attentive care. But, in fact, can God stand back and still intervene when things go wrong? Does God, Jesus, the Holy Spirit come to our aid when we stray, sin, or fall sick? Can he do so without intruding on our freedom? Does he respond to our prayers about such things, and if so do Christians get a better deal than others? Foolish questions, perhaps, but near to the heart of us all when terror strikes. Do our bleating prayers make any difference, or does God respect our freedom to wander where we will, and continue to lean against a tree just watching us, playing his pipes to himself?

To take it a stage further, how does God – if he does intervene – balance the needs of the individual sheep with the needs of the whole flock? In the other parable about sheep off goes the shepherd to look for the stray, leaving the flock behind. And is our freedom merely freedom only as long as we don't go beyond the bounds laid down?

To summarize the problems. A simple picture of a shepherd and his flock, which Jesus paints, raises problems about God's care. Does he intervene if necessary? How does he choose when and when not to do so? How does he balance indvidual needs with those of the community and greatest of all what degree of freedom do we have? Total, or just what God thinks is good for us? And thrown into that is the question, does prayer make a difference to the outcome of it all?

All that is certainly worth contemplating for an hour or so, though there are of course no answers. The only partial answer we have is by looking at the Cross. Here is the perfect balance of all things. Perfect stillness and perfect action. With scarcely a word spoken, without movement or doing, without a dying instruction, Christ watches his creation from the tree and God's greatest work is achieved. God does not intervene to save his Son, but the Cross is his eternal intervention and pattern of divine 'intrusion' to save inanimate and animate creation. Peter Baelz, the scholarly Dean of Durham, wrote a little book entitled 'Does God answer prayer?' The question wasn't answered as such, but we knew more about the nature of God, as part of our prayers, by the time we reached the last page. That nature only intrudes in the eternal appeal of the perfect expression of love seen in the shepherd on the Cross. That is what goes out to find the sheep, that is what leaves us completely free yet is sacrificially caring. That is God-in-Christ's appealing prayer for his people.

Scientists and philosophers tell us about the importance at times of assuming that a certain law or principle is not true, doubting it, and seeing where that leads. Doubting the possibility of God's intervention into the world and seeing where that takes us, is as important as assuming that he does gently push his way in. If I had to define prayer, or part of it anyway, I would say it is an exploration into the nature of God and what is brought about by that exploration. We see God at work; we see God's nature most beautifully, most riskily, most open to all, when we explore and excavate God, his world and ourselves in the light of the crucified darkness. We can then do none other than adore, confess, plead and give thanks.

One other point about the parable, 'I am the Good Shepherd'. The word 'good' in its Greek context can mean 'good to look at'. Beautiful in outward form, and even in the way a person walks, dances and so on. It was also a word the Greeks used in their graffiti. It was written on trees and walls with the name of their lover attached. A rather attractive thought. The graffiti of heart, mind and soul. Clearly it was used in the moral sense, a virtuous sense, but in a way that had strength about it. Tough, something against which evil and ugliness could not triumph. Such is the Good Shepherd.

I don't think, however, that I am stretching my language to the limit if I suggest that the word 'good' could mean 'good at the job'. Skilful and profitable at the job. We have here a shepherd in whom we can have confidence. I like my doctor to be a good person, but above all I require him to be skilful, to know what he's about. Keen on knowing his medicine thoroughly. Though I don't think that morality necessarily alters a person's skill at their job. It is skill that is primary.

Our Lord is a professional shepherd and knows the job through and through. He gave plenty of evidence that he did. Done in his case with perfect purity even if he were in the eyes of the Jewish authorities an 'immoral' person. He 'blasphemed', particularly during his trial, and consorted with sinners, and the Jews had a high doctrine of moral rub-off. In him we have the pure professional, skilled in that job of watchfulness, tending, guiding, freedom-conferring, to flock and individuals alike.

A brief coda. 'The good shepherd lays down his life for the sheep', the parable tells us. But here is a doubling of roles. For not only is Jesus the good shepherd, he is also the slaughtered Lamb of God who takes away the sins of the world. The parables, and that is another characteristic of them, are great history-recallers. They bring to mind the history of Israel. Marvellously, movingly so. Jesus as the shepherd recalls the patriarchs, those first great shepherds of the nation. Moses who is summoned by God as he tends his flock by the burning bush. David the archetypal shepherd, both in reality and as leader of Israel and Judah. 'He chose David also his servant and took him away from the sheep-folds. As he was following the ewes he took him, that he might feed Jacob his people and Israel his inheritance.' All symbols of shepherding under the power of God. Yet the slaughtered lamb of the Passover, with its blood upon the door lintel, is the symbol of the exodus, the freeing of Israel from slavery, and their eventual entry into the promised land. Isaiah uses such sacrificial symbolism too. John the Baptist labels Jesus as the Lamb of God. What Jesus represents, through the Cross he also redeems. He joins the historical concept of community and leadership with the symbolism of the lamb in Jewish history. All redeemed and joined in his Cross and Passion.

So hidden in the parable of Jesus the Good Shepherd is a wealth of word pictures, a gold-mine of difficulties, and a treasure of mysteries. Wonderful for meditation and discussion.

7

The Vineyard

St Mark 12: 1–9

Lectures by most theologians are not Royal Albert Hall fillers but not long ago a bearded, Merlin-like bishop held a hall full of Cornish clergy enthralled with the nature of God. It was a three-line-whip occasion, part of what is called Continuing Ministerial Education, a name which is enough to persuade those hard-working priests to discover an urgent hospital visit or a sudden funeral for that day. But the vast majority came and were entranced.

I haven't his brilliance with words or his command of spotlight phrases but essentially what the lecturer said was this: the Gospels are not in essence a record of some events that took place in an obscure corner of the Roman Empire two thousand years ago, let alone the biography of a skilful story-telling carpenter who met a sticky end. They are, he told us, the exploration of a crater after a divine explosion. A world-shattering event which makes any dinosaur-destroying meteorite look puny in its effect. What the Gospel writers do, what the whole New Testament does, is pick up the pieces of the bomb, some sharp and still warm bits of shrapnel, and ask us if a piece large or small of the bomb looks and feels like this, if it is constructed in such and such a way, what does it tell us about the mind of the maker? If this were the temperature of the epicentre of the explosion, what does it tell us about the temperature of the furnace from which it came? What does it tell us of the skill and intentions of the bomb-making engineer? And all further illuminated by the marks that were left on the crater and the effect the explosion had on the surroundings.

The theologian peeled off layer after layer of this onion-like bomb, revealing the nature of the crater and sent us away inspired to do some exploring ourselves.

I would contend that some of the hottest bomb blast bits, some of the most evocative and thrilling pieces of shrapnel, some of the sharpest chunks of metal, some of the most revealing imprints in the walls of the crater, are the parables. They compel us to ask, what do they show us about the nature of God? We may not be able to answer in a straightforward statement, something that could be translated into Latin, and such a difficulty has given theologians work and excitement down the ages. More likely our revelations will be the knowing of our prayers, and the changing of our deeds, a depicting in love and action of that crater and the pieces we found in it. But that is often the most convincing evidence for our shell-shock. There is an odd verse in one of the psalms, which I am told is not in the Hebrew original, translated in the Book of Common Prayer as, 'One deep calleth to another, because of the noise of the waterpipes'. I've never heard any convincing description of its meaning, but I find it rather a good definition of intercessory prayer and the nature and effect of parable. God's depths vibrating with our depths because of some mundane matter or other. And the same applies to the parables. They light up the depths of the nature of God which resound with the depths of our nature, and they do it through the telling of an ordinary story or in some cases a not-so-ordinary story. They explore more than most parts of Scripture the centre of the divine explosive intervention.

All of which I ask you to bear in mind as I take you through the parable of the Vineyard as recorded by St Mark. One of the briefest of parables, but one where the bomb bits are at their hottest and the pieces most jagged – almost unbearably so. It is perhaps the parable most immersed in Scripture, most resonant with scriptural themes, and the one most obviously connected with the Passion.

The Parable

Vineyards and gardens were close to the Jewish heart and close to the heart of Jewish history. Naboth's vineyard speaks of ownership and plunder, as does this parable. The human tendency when dealing with all natural things is to mix tenancy and responsibility with possession. Isaiah, Chapter 5 is almost identical with the parable and aimed at the Jewish people who failed in their duty of producing the things designed by God for their mutual joy. There are verses in that

book of love, the Song of Solomon, which speak of vines, and St
Bernard of Clairvaux used the verse in the book, 'The little foxes that
spoil the vines', when preaching to his crowded noviciate in his mon-
astery. All these passages show how humanity takes the risk of sinful
and stupid arrogance and God swamps it with his own daring. The
swamping risk of love and creative ownership.

This parable despite its brevity carries on this heart-rending theme.
Written into it is the timeless nature of God's continual goodness.
The chorus of mankind's wickedness and the chorus of God's generosity. God's offer of himself, without limit and withholding. The
parable has echoes of nearly every part of Scripture, the psalms, the
prophets, Genesis, even the history books. We do not know who
wrote Mark's Gospel, but he certainly knew how to create vibrations
of Hebrew history for his readers. The longest unbroken psalm, Psalm
78, for instance, has as a chorus 'and yet he forgave their misdeeds',
God trying again and again. A theme which makes the parable what
it is.

Like so many vineyard stories this one has a tragic inevitability
about it. The tragedy of – why? Why go on sending those servants let
alone his son? The whole thing makes no sense at all. If it weren't for
the way that it is told it would be considered merely a silly tale. But it
lights up the whole of the Gospel story which is about God in Christ
seemingly acting stupidly. We expect him to act like a sensible,
rational human being, and he doesn't. Sensible human beings don't
turn the other cheek. Sensible human beings don't consider poverty
a happier state than riches. Mark doesn't try to tidy up the madness of
God. The folly of God penetrates beyond our thinking, as St Paul
realized personally on the road to Damascus, and waxes poetical
about it at the beginning of his first letter to the Corinthians. Lent
should be such a time of re-thought folly.

But back to my first characteristic of parables – beauty. There is an
overwhelming beauty of pathos in the story. A pathos of hope that is
impossibly hopeless, yet like the beauty of Passion narrative you still
feel each time you read it that perhaps those involved will respond.
Perhaps the Jews and Pilate will understand and release their Lord.
Perhaps the tenants will rejoice to obey their master. It has the beauty
of inevitability, like a Greek tragedy where we know in our heart that
the whole thing is unstoppable. Such is the Passion story.

The thing, however, that fascinates me is the contrasting of beauty
with ugliness. The actions of the owner of the vineyard shimmer in

beauty and the tenants have a feeling of ugliness, of a distorted form of wickedness about them. The first is a beauty that compels and the latter an ugliness which repels. Again, I see that contrast written into the whole of the Gospel and often written into the parables. Christ has a beauty about his presence, and his opponents a contrasting ugliness, all skilfully pictured by the Gospel writers, even the legalistic Matthew. But, alas, by the time we enter parts of the Acts of the Apostles, and particularly when we enter the commandment-ridden parts of some of the Epistles, the coloured, free-flying butterfly of Christ has been pinned to the display board. 'Twas ever thus, as the Franciscans have often borne witness. Paul was dealing with the ugliness of sin, but it is worth a Lent meditation to ponder whether his ways of responding to that ugliness didn't sometimes pile more ugliness on to it in sharp contrast to the method of hope and beauty we find in this parable.

To take it a stage further, are beauty and ugliness reflected in heart, mind and soul better criteria for judging the morality of people and situations than codes of conduct? How does the history of our faith from the post-Gospel New Testament onwards, square with the beauty of the nature of God as seen in this parable and the events of the Passion and crucifixion?

And what about risk? Obviously there is the risk of creation and its purpose. We have a Lord who expects something from his creation. Not because he is a grasping landlord but because by realizing its purpose, creation is reflecting what it was made for. Made for and fashioned for, as St Augustine enchantingly insists. Created for the glory of God. I have a feeling that vines are happier when they have produced a good crop of grapes. When the wine is a vintage year. God has risked his plans to us, and if we do not realize them his joy in us is saddened and so is our joy in him and his creation. The slaughtering of the landlord's son becomes inevitable, for the vineyard represents that joyful unity between humankind and the rest of creation, and God is willing to risk his own being realized in his Son to make good that glorious unity. We can only really be happy when we have cultivated and returned to God what is his own. His own is given to us on trust, not merely on loan, a distinction which is desperately important if we are to be adult tenants.

But the concept I find most moving of all is that little phrase 'They will reverence my son'. What inconceivable, total foolishness. If we were in that position where we had sent various people to bring back the rent on our property and they been molested and bullied, we would send in the bailiffs backed up by the boys in blue, not send our gentle precious child. That would be the height of craziness. It is sheer madness. And always in the heart of God there is this utterly foolish beseeching of his creation. 'They will repent. I am sure they will when they see that I am putting my ultimate trust in them.' The beseeching of the humility of God. A beseeching reflected in Jesus's betrayal by Judas. It wasn't a policy difference between them that eventually led to treason. It was the humble acceptance of a woman risking her wealth and pouring out that box of precious ointment over him, with the usual rejoinder that is ever made when jealousy invades the generosity of love. 'It could have been sold and the money given to the poor.' That is what led to betrayal. Jesus is asking the disciples to see that the woman's risk, risking her most precious possession, is a reflection of God doing the same in him. Judas couldn't take such foolishness. Off he goes to betray a Lord whose God he finds too foolish to follow. And the Cross shouts at us, 'They will reverence my Son'. This beseeching in all its stupidity is written into the divine nature. It is the hottest piece of shrapnel of all in that eternal explosion. Such giving is the heartbeat of God, and his Son is a mad accomplice in this scheme of redemption.

I mentioned the word 'precious' in the last paragraph. That is perhaps the heart of the biblical theme in this parable. Central to the risky thinking in the Bible is the sacrifice of the most precious. It is pivotal to the Bible from beginning to end. Abraham leaving his lands and home for the unknown; but most of all his offering up of Isaac, his precious. David has that glorious phrase, 'I will not offer to God that which has cost me nothing'. The prophets give their most precious all, and the disciples eventually see that their most precious thinking must go. Likewise St Paul, who counts it all as dung. The readiness to offer our most precious is central to our faith and without it I doubt whether we can ever become what God would have us be. It was and still is the hallmark of the saints.

The good Lord took risk after risk with the Jewish law and with Jewish morality, and the parable describes the reward he got for it. His association with the outcast and so-called immoral, his condemnation of the officials, of the rich and the righteous – all those things that Jesus knew, to use the vineyard metaphor, prevented the tenants from giving back to others the glorious fruits of the Jewish religious orchard.

People kindly put at the bottom of letters they write to me or my brother, 'Take care'. I'm never quite sure what I am meant to be careful about, though I appreciate their concern. My brother often writes back: 'No, no, take risks'.

Lastly the ending of the parable. Can we really believe it was part of the original story as told by Jesus, and borrowed from Isaiah? The punishment of those who beat the landlord's agents and then killed his son? It doesn't make sense in the light of the rest of the parable and it makes no sense at all in the light of the Cross. But the whole Bible is riddled with divine vengeance, which again is difficult to square with what we know of the nature of God as seen in Christ. The modern world uses the word 'retribution' to justify such vengeance, when all it means in effect is 'revenge'. Can punishment really be part of the nature of a completely loving God who risks all? Have we got a God who in the end says enough is enough and awards us our deserts, our come-uppance? Does sin and wickedness need punishment before it can be swamped with the love and risk of God? I do not know, but I do know that punishment is usually ineffective, and love is not. I do know that punishment is ugly and in the end makes the awarders of it ugly too. Forgiveness and love are beautiful and I am not convinced that punishment is part of that forgiveness. But I do know that it is forgiveness that often produces repentance, not punishment. So I have difficulty squaring a beautiful, complete though open-ended parable with the ugly ending.

So when you read and think about this parable, which like all parables contains within it the pattern of human nature and the pattern of God's response, think about the beauty and risk that is contained within it, and risk thinking the impossible as far as your own behaviour is concerned. As someone has said, our casting out of the precious Son from that vineyard is not a violent affair. We drive him out with indifference, with carelessness, with protective routines, and with ugliness. But there can be no beauty, no mystery and the breaking-down of the hedges round God's glorious gardens without risk and wonderful foolishness.

8

The Prodigal Son

St Luke 15: 11–32

Shakespeare is out of fashion in schools they tell us. Out of date, and to give it the final destroying label, boring. The language is too difficult. The action too slow. The story dull and not soap-like enough. The past is the past, they add. For me, however, the Shakespearean corpus and the Bible are essential volumes in the library on my desert island. Shakespeare loves to tackle the fundamentals of human nature and clothe them with gripping drama. The fatal flaws of mankind that inevitably lead to tragedy. Many of his plays are parables – explorations into the nature of men and women with their passions and vices; their virtues and loves.

One of the things that fascinates and heightens their appeal to all ages, ages of people as well as down the ages, is they appear to have no beginning and often no ending. They seem to be plucked out of time. The plot and the verse were there already, and all Shakespeare had to do was find them and write them down. A bit like a statue of St Cuthbert in the cloisters of Durham Cathedral made out of a tree that was blown down on the green. St Cuthbert appears to have been hiding in the tree all the time, just waiting to be released.

Likewise with Shakespeare, we are in on a month or two, a few years perhaps, in the life of the characters in the story, a story which has been going on before we arrived and will continue after we have departed. We are observers on the lives and actions of a historical verbal opera, that is as real, and mind- and heart-opening, as if it were happening for the first time. Happening before our eyes and ears and will go on happening when we have stopped watching and listening. That is what gives the drama power, that is what stimulates our hearts, minds and tear-ducts, that is what makes us wish it were possible to alter the course of action, to leap into the play and shout 'No! This shall not happen!' Change the source of the story so the heartbreak is avoided. Change history so the Ides of March are no longer fatal for Caesar, so that Macbeth's ambition is restrained, Lear's madness calmed.

In the same way, a parable does its job. The story is part of life. A snapshot, a story slot with something that could happen in one form or other, anywhere, any time, that has already begun and will continue when Jesus has finished telling his tale. They have both a 'centred in time' quality and yet a timelessness about them. As with a Shakespearean play, or any good drama, they make us want to take part, affect the story, and be affected by it. Tell the priest and Levite, in the parable of the Good Samaritan, what we think of them and their appalling avoidance of the wounded traveller. Take action against the tenants of the Vineyard who have battered the rent collectors of the lord. Shout, 'Why?' to the king who binds the guest who has no wedding garment, and casts him out, even though 'morning dress' may have been available free at the door. We wish to interfere, such is the 'be-there' of the story.

And that, above all, is the feeling behind the Prodigal Son. Not that we wish in this case to interfere, perhaps, but the tale is so powerful, so real, that we wish to be in on the rejoicing, the penitence of the prodigal, and the pathos of the elder brother. We love to embrace the story and become one of the characters. Have a walk-on part in the drama at the very least. That is what I suspect the crowds meant when they felt that Jesus taught with authority, and not like the scribes and Pharisees. Somehow or other they knew that the author of the story was in touch with the author of all things, with the God of reality who lay behind his teachings.

Those feelings of timelessness, of being in on it, of authority, are strongest and most tangible, of course, in the parable of the Passion. We have only to read it, listen to it sung in the music of Bach, to realize that it still continues. It has no beginning or ending. It is both completed and still doing its work. It is never to be repeated, but 'shown forth day by day' as a eucharistic hymn puts it. We wish to be there. We need to be there, as we do in the ordinary parables.

Above all, despite Christ being the victim, he is also the person of authority in the death drama, as much as he was when he told those tales of the Kingdom. 'The Kingdom of Heaven is like this', as he often says before telling a parable. Indeed it is like this as the Passion unfolds. Despite his bonds, his wounds, the story gives the impression that though he is powerless, he is somehow in charge. He appears to be the person with freedom while the others are in chains. Like one of the productions I saw of Richard II, which made him as he sat on the cell floor seem Christ-like. Bonded yet free.

Two other points before I say something in more detail about perhaps the greatest of all parables, the Prodigal Son. In most Shakespearean tragedies and histories we not only have a characteristic of humanity lit up for us – overweening ambition in Macbeth; jealous and passionate love in Othello; the pathos of old age in Lear, and so on – Shakespeare, as well, lighting up such characteristics, the things that make us tick, shows us relentlessly where those natures of humanity can lead. The plays are not only parables of identification, they are plays about the forces unleashed by those identified features hidden in us all, lurking beneath the surface and where their unleashing would take us.

In Shakespeare, however, there is rarely redemption, despite some Victorian additions and adaptations to the plays to produce a happy ending. But Jesus in his Passion and death, and finally in his resurrection, not only redeems those identified characteristics, he also redeems the powers, and the total possibilities revealed by them. Not only the powers themselves but the road those powers take. Peter's treachery is redeemed every step of the way. 'The Lord turned and looked upon Peter.' Jesus collects the rubbish and all that has been polluted on the road, and takes it to the purification plant of Calvary. His diagnosis, prognosis and cure are achieved. Perhaps all that is worth a Lenten meditation or two. Yes, Jesus and Shakespeare and great artists in general are the great diagnosticians of humanity. That is their job. Perhaps being wounded people is a preliminary to that ability. They diagnose the weaknesses, the diseases of heart and mind and body in humanity, give us the prognosis and by their art point to the possibility of changing redemption. A redemption seen in the Cross and Passion of our Lord.

Before I tackle the parable itself, my other point is this. The characteristics which Shakespeare identifies, the ambition of Macbeth, for instance, gradually, and in his case fatally, separates that character from his fellow men and women. When the play opens, Macbeth is one of the boys, at ease with his fellow soldiers and lords. But as his terrible ambition takes over, and demands more and more, so separation inevitably follows. Fear of being betrayed, or supplanted, consumes him and in the end he is alone, no longer able to communicate or be alongside his former companions. Lear is a symbol of loneliness. Caesar is immune to danger, separate, and God-like, and in the end must fall. The weaknesses of them all not only destroys them, but detroys the unity of the community around them.

Christ in his Passion takes that separation, becomes that separation, and in his utter and final loneliness on the Cross redeems it. He breaks down the deep gulf which our mortal selfish passions have dug out for us, and recreates them, reforms them to bridge that gulf. As St Anselm says, 'Thou hast created me and re-created me, thou hast formed me and reformed me.' The unity of the personal and the unity of the community become one through the Passion. It is one of the benefits of the Passion. Something that we can feel and sense within family and friends. The restored unity which the prodigal has with his father.

The Parable

And so to the parable itself, which the medievals called the summary of the Gospel. The Gospel in one. The Gospel in a single story. It contains just about all. It reveals most completely our Lord's teaching on the nature of God. Its beauty is almost tangible. It leaps out of the frame. It enchants in every word, except in one or two of the modern translations. The mixture of Christ's and Luke's telling is a master-piece of unified writing. How was it done? In the studio of Christ's mind as he prayed. If genius is 90 per cent perspiration and 10 per cent inspiration, the dividing line here and the proportions are perfect. It is one of the parables that creates awe, and the imagination immediately creates the scene. Likewise the risk element. The father's risk in giving the younger son his inheritance. The utterly stupid risk of the son in its use. The risk of the welcome back. The risk of antagonizing the elder brother, and so on. There is open-endedness too, an incompleteness in the finale to the parable. Nothing is worked through. We are not told what happens to the younger son. Does he become the good guy? Did the elder brother come in to the party and embrace him? What was the outcome of it all? It is a scene out of family life that began before that parable is told and goes on after it is finished.

Let me come to the parable slantwise, and talk first of all about agreements. The world works by, depends on, agreements, usually about things or status. The big agreement in life is that you don't normally get something for nothing. You get something for something, and nothing for nothing. So the world works. Likewise status. The world works by agreements about goods and status and runs for litigation when it feels diddled.

Agreements of this kind are written large in this parable, but like so many parables there is a twist in the tail. The younger brother had probably worked for his father. He had given his father something, and he was his son. So as far as ordinary thinking was concerned he was entitled to something in return. He asked for it and his father did not refuse. No conditions were made. Off he went having turned it all into ready money. And the same applied in the far country after a life on the razzle and supplies were exhausted. He hired himself out to the local piggery. He got something for something, his work, even if it were a pittance. The same applied to his intentions when he came to his senses and realized there was no other way than to return home. 'If I ask for work perhaps my father will give me a wage.' Something for something, even if he had ceased to have expectations of being somebody. He no longer thought he would have the status of his sonship. 'I am no longer worthy to be called your son. Let's have an agreement as a servant', he thinks as he trudges home.

But, wonder of wonders, that is not the way his father works. He is watching, waiting, and he dashes out as soon as the dust on the horizon stirs. He won't even allow his son to finish the prepared, rehearsed agreement speech. Out comes everything for nothing. Scholars have found all sorts of symbolism in the clothes and gifts that were brought out, but the restoration was beyond wildest dreams. He gets more than something for nothing. He is restored to more than just anybody. All the usual agreement rules are broken. The rules of ordinary, standard right thinking, fair, just behaviour are cast aside. No wonder the elder brother is enraged. No wonder he won't come into the house.

And what is the father's reaction to that? 'My son, all that I have is thine.' In other words, don't you realize that we are partners in the estate management? We are sharers in the whole enterprise. So, do you not want to share in this particular piece of restoration work as well? This home-coming? Would you prefer to be an agreement-man rather than a son? A sharer in a humility home-coming or a just deserts man?

Although it may sound far-fetched, and perhaps far-fetchedness is yet another feature of parables, this turning of normal practice upside down is the wonder of the Passion. Though God needs no persuading, the Passion breaks all the agreement rules. All petty thinking on roles disappear. He breaks the old rule, for instance, that repentance is required – just as the Prodigal may have been repentant, but it was not required for restoration. The Passion demonstrates that agreements in the legal sense of the word are over. The New Covenant in Christ's blood is completely one-sided. There is all for nothing. We had gone into a far country, but God's Son also identifies himself *as* the Prodigal, rather than just *with* the Prodigal, and joins us there. He joins us utterly in the mire and in the death of sonship, which the Prodigal appears to undergo, and persuades us home by that identification. He is present in the whole parable. He is the actor of the parts on our behalf. I have some reservations about the theology of Christ's Passion and dying being instead of us rather than on our behalf. Nasty atonement theories of penal substitution to satisfy a wrathful God come rushing forward if we use 'instead of' rather than 'on our behalf from sheer love'. Why we have to allot just a set of human emotions to God rather than 'emotions' that are completely beyond our understanding, I do not know. I have to be persuaded that the need for retribution is written into the universe as some atonement theories imply. God's justice and satisfaction are not within our understanding except that love is paramount, and as St Augustine said, and he was certainly a prodigal, 'Perfect justice implies a plenitude of mercy'. Human justice bears little resemblance, I suspect, to God's. Normal agreements, normal covenants, are over, and our status is restored free gratis.

He casts aside his clothing in the Passion on our behalf so that the Father can reclothe us in the best garments; as St Paul says, the garments that suit God's chosen people. We no longer even need to begin our speech of agreement. Christ has made it for us and we are restored as sons. The parable, too, is a picture of the resurrection feast. Good Friday may be God's dancing day but it is we, the parable makes clear, who get the new shoes to walk in his courts and dance his dance. The sadness of 'righteousness' will be overcome by that music which the Father and the Son through the Spirit ever play afresh.

One more point. It is the longing in the parable that I find most moving of all. The longing by the father for the return of the

prodigal. The longing for generosity by the elder brother. And longing is at the centre of the Passion. It hangs there beseeching us with
no strings attached. It is the same longing that we found in the
parable of the Vineyard when the owner sent his son to the tenants.

There is a church in one of our larger cities which stands fairly
vandalized in a poor and run-down area of the city. A lad who had
been a server there in his youth fell into bad company in his late
teens, and left the Church. Finally he ended up murdering someone
from a rival gang and was sent to prison for life. Because of his age
and surroundings the sentence was commuted to manslaughter and
he was released after seven years. It was a Sunday morning when he
arrived back in his home city and he wandered the streets not knowing where to go. He passed the church where he had been a server,
and thought he would creep in and stand at the back for a few
minutes. At least it was warmer inside. As he entered, the priest was
just saying the Peace before the Offertory inviting people to
exchange a sign of that peace. The congregation turned round to see
who had come in and the ex-prisoner retreated into the shadows in
case he were recognized. And recognized he was. The whole congregation surrounded him, embracing him and welcoming him home.
The old priest took him to the vestry and clothed him in his white
alb and took him into the sanctuary to serve, as he had before he
went into a far country.

9

A Meditation on the Passion

St Mark 8: 27

This text, 'Whom do men say that I am?', is usually taken as the lead-up to the great declaration of faith by St Peter, which Jesus got out of him by asking the right questions. Jesus, confident about his mission and messiahship. A clarion call, a knowing of his mission and purpose. But I wonder. It could be equally taken as Jesus having an identity crisis. Jesus full of doubt and questioning about his own status, his relationship to his Father, his mission and purpose. His need to ask questions about himself.

I find that quite amazing and even more wonderful and cheering than any clarion call. Here is the Son of God. Here is our human-shaped gospel, who needs and looks for an affirmation, a propping up, by his circle of friends. Here is our Saviour who is so at one with our humanity that instead of being confidently above our weakness, he shares it. He shares our need for reassurance from those he loves. We have no British stiff upper lip, but one who shares our fragility and our tremblingness about his faith, his nature, his purpose. Incredible.

And such is writ large in the Gospels. Such trembling, such doubt is central. The temptations are a reflection of it, assailings of Christ's need to test God's confidence in him. His change of direction in Gospel method, his agony in the garden, his cry of searing doubt – 'My God, my God, why hast thou forsaken me?' – from the Cross are the nails of doubt, the spear of self-fragility. We have here no above-our-mortality Lord. Not, as we hear in that line in a Christmas carol, a 'No crying he makes' Saviour, but one who shares every cry of agony, of doubt, darkness and fear. He shares all that is human. Amazing. Amazing that he allows humanity through his question 'Whom do men say that I am?', to gaze on those glorious scars of doubt.

But what about us? It seems to me in this time when evangelism and mission are near the top of many Christian lists that it is essential, desperate, that we preach a Gospel, a faith, that is fully human. So that must include doubt, which is part of our own and our Lord's human condition. Such doubt is certainly not the opposite to faith. On the contrary it is part of it. If we, instead, throw a 'We have all the answers, we have the certainties' faith at our fellow men and women, how can we share their shadows and hopes? How can we enter into their trembling humanity? How can we show them a fully human Saviour? The blasting gunfire of absolutes is no Gospel, no Good News, but merely a throwing of hand grenades that makes people run for their shelters and their ear-plugs.

For the wonder of doubt is that it immediately throws us back on God instead of on our own confidence. We realize that we cannot go it alone. Doubt leads inevitably to obedience, as it did for Christ, and leads to self-examination of our love and discipleship. Doubt is the route to freedom and service, unlike self-confident faith which is a cul-de-sac to sterility. For the wonder of it all is that we know – which is our only confidence – that our own hesitations, our own tremblings, because of Christ, are part of God himself.

So I implore you, have no fear of your fears. Tremble not at your tremblings. Continue the quest of questioning. For if Christ himself can say, 'Whom do men say that I am?' not sure of the answer save that it will be found through a Cross, we can assuredly find confidence in his doubt. We can find hope in his trembling fears. We can find such certainty as we need in his fragility, and in his dark death we can find our daily resurrections.

10

A Meditation on 'I am the door'

St John 10: 7–9

A short meditation on the other picture Jesus uses about himself in John's tenth chapter. A rather more tricky picture on the imagination than that of the Good Shepherd. Many artists have painted Jesus as the Good Shepherd. I know of none who have depicted him as a Door. A bit of semantics to begin with. The word in verse 6 often translated as 'parable' is a different Greek word from that used for 'parable' in the other Gospels. Although it can have much the same meaning, it also has a more enigmatic quality about it. It can mean a mysterious saying, a word which is a boxful of words all rolled into one. I love such words. You can open the box and let them fly out. But no wonder they were puzzled by it all, and verses 8 and 9 increase the bewilderment. Some Christians have used those verses to claim the total supremacy of Christianity over all other faiths and Christ as the only possible doorway to the Kingdom of God.

A famous Cambridge theologian of the first half of the last century used to say to his students, 'Bury your head in a Greek lexicon and you will arise in the presence of God'. As you probably know, a lexicon isn't a straightforward Greek dictionary. For one thing it is only one way. Greek into English. It is also an etymological dictionary, and one that shows how a particular word was used by Greek authors of antiquity. For instance, look up the Greek word meaning 'to follow' and you discover it also means 'accompany' and 'copy', with usages to prove it. Though that is a fairly obvious one. The Greek word for 'door', too, has some wonderful uses and contexts which would probably have been known to the writer of John's Gospel even if they weren't to Jesus, who may or may not have spoken popular Greek.

It can, for instance, mean the place where people brought their petitions. When the letter to the Ephesians says 'through Christ we have access to God' Paul is talking about such a door. The door-keeper would have collected those petitions and taken them to the master of the house, who would have granted or denied or perhaps postponed those requests. Christ is both the door and the keeper, who bundles up our petitions and takes them suitably embellished with love to the ever-loving Father. Such is the Servant King.

The word can also be a metaphor for the place where disciples waited on famous teachers. They would wait at the door for the master to emerge and deliver his wisdom, and answer their difficult questions. It is a lovely thought that a follower of a Rabbi should be so anxious to hear his master's voice that he stood there for hours desperate to collect those sayings that could alter his mind and heart. As the psalmist says, 'I waited patiently for the Lord'. The students stood thrilled by the subtleties of the teacher's mind. No wonder that the word for door can also mean the entrance into a person's soul. So Jesus the Door is the gate to our hearts and minds and we to his.

The door to our health of body too. The sheep-fold was usually a courtyard in front of the house. The sheep were brought into it for the night. As the sheep and goats came in, the shepherds not only sorted out those of their own flock (several flocks often gathered in one fold) but they also checked them over for damage or disease. Jesus the Door is the place where tending takes place, and not only is he the entrance into health of body, mind and spirit, he is also the producer and doctor of all three.

William Temple, in his wonderful book, *Readings in St John's Gospel*, distinguishes in what seems now a slightly old-fashioned way between the sheep, the laity whose pasture is outside the fold, i.e., in the world, and the clergy whose work is 'religion' inside the fold (the Church). Both equal members of the fold and both inhabiting pasture and fold but distinguished by their different emphases. Now-adays the two are a total jumble and in many ways rightly so. The two jobs – clerical and lay – are not as separate as was once thought, though there are valid and needful differences in nature of function and caring, and Jesus being both shepherd and Lamb of God stands amongst and is part of both.

But it is the sharp divide some Christians make between their Christian work and their secular work that I find difficult. The accountant or butcher who comes home from work and when he has thrown away his brief-case or apron, dons his Christian thinking and goes out to do his visiting of the sick, leading a Bible study group, partaking in a prayer posse, all of which he assumes are somehow more Christian than his sums or sirloins, are my difficulty.

What we really need are people who are not Christians who happen to be butchers or teachers, but Christians who discover by prayer and thought (if there is any difference in this case), by study and discussion, what it means to be a Christian accountant, nurse, teacher or labourer. People who have an understanding of how to make their patch of pasture green with Christian goodness, and who have made their work and their faith one. Likewise clergy who have made a study, often in their study, of what is involved in being a Christian actuary or baker and prayerfully offering these people and their jobs to God. Such study by laity and clergy is desperately needed if the people in the world and the functioning of the world is to be made holy. These men and women are not more 'Christian-jobby' when they are sick visiting armed with their Bibles than they are when they are dashing round the ward armed with their hypodermic, or a butcher with his cleaver. At the moment we need a greater awareness of what it means to be Christian in our particular pasture, than what it means to be Christian in the fold. Masters may come to look like their dogs. We need sheep in the field who have come to look like the shepherd.

Two other points in this short meditational chapter. One straightforward and one very difficult even to discuss. First the ultimate door for the Jewish family was the Passover one with the blood of a lamb smeared upon it. Reminding them yearly of their flight from Egypt and the sparing of their first-born sons from the death that killed the first-born of the Egyptians. Reminding them of their privileges and responsibilities as a chosen people whom God would guide to the Promised Land and forever claim as his own. And Christians have seen all this as a prefiguring of Christ, the sacrificial Lamb. That blood upon the lintel of the fold sanctifies our going out into God's world and coming into his Church. It is the door through which the Church on behalf of God blesses his world and receives that world into his arms. The door where divine grace and response are the same thing.

Secondly, some would say Christ is the only door to the Kingdom of Heaven and there is no other way to salvation. Of course, Christ is not only the door but also the way to that door, the salvation highway, and we through our Christ-likeness are part of that road. But if men and women are not attracted to that door, or if they are and do not knock, the Christian community is as much to blame as they are, and it is not for us to be judgemental. We simply do not know what held them back. We have to realize, too, that John's Gospel is one of extreme contrasts, written for a world where as well as much goodness there were cultic and moral horrors. Grey areas were not for him.

One or two other points on this particular difficulty, centred on Jerusalem. Jerusalem is where the redemption of the whole world is played out on a Cross smeared with blood as was the lintel of those doors. But Jerusalem is also the focal point of the world's three monotheistic faiths. Jerusalem is the interlocking of faiths and their fulfilment. But the Christian way of redemption acted out there through suffering and resurrection lies in the powerlessness of God, not in his power, and because of that it not only says but also does something in a mysterious way for all those faiths. Weakness not supremacy is at the centre of our faith, our preaching and mission and cannot exclude anyone, whatever the outward appearance might show. It flows over, both within Jerusalem and also outside the city of God. Response to the call of Jerusalem can take many forms, seen and unseen.

So two points from this short mishmash on Christ the Door, which might be worth discussing. First, how we work out the inter-weaving and relationship of our job and our faith. Secondly, how we preach Christ the Door and also, as the Book of Revelation makes clear, Christ the Key. Christ did not mince his words to the Pharisees about such matters. If we somehow put others off by our life and words, those who are wanting to creep with hesitancy towards that door, we may find that we are among a fair number of proclaiming, committed Christians standing outside.

11

The Pearl of Great Price
St Matthew 13: 44–46

Jesus is the master craftsman, the supreme exhibitor, of treasure-hunting skills. And perhaps his greatest craftsmanship in teaching and preaching, which in him merge into one, are his sculptured parables. You can sense the excitement as the story is told. Often as in this case a story that was current at the time, or one of the old or new fables circulating in the community. There are other versions of these parables, one of them contained in the Gospel of Thomas. But you can almost hear the gasp of amazement as Jesus re-forms it with electric effect and gives it a final and completely different twist. You know in his telling that unlike that of the scribes and Pharisees he has penetrated the soft spots in their armour.

You have no doubt that in those early morning prayer sessions, described in St Mark's Gospel, when he gives us a day in the life of the Lord, that Jesus has sweated over his lesson, trembled at his sermon, at the words he felt compelled to lay before the crowds. He has made the old new, and hearts are revitalized, bewildered or, alas, repelled. Some will take it away and make it their treasure for life. Many of those parables may be Jewish tales resurrected by Jesus. But they are not just given a new coat of paint, they are reworked and re-carved. Lazarus and Dives is another one. And again, the genie of excitement comes out of the repolished and recast old lamp. He has made someone else's story his own, something which lies at the heart of these crafts. The style of the master comes through at every phrase and you can tell at once when it is not his own, as in the explanation of the parable of the Sower.

There comes, however, a point, a terrifying point in many ministries whether they be private or public, when it becomes apparent that hearts and minds and souls can only be changed by a sacrificial living-out of that preaching and teaching. Where the treasures of the parables spoken must become the painfully lived-out ones. There is no other way forward. There came a Rubicon where, though Jesus knew he was continuing to enchant them, the message of who he was and what his work was had failed to penetrate the leaders, the disciples and the crowd. The precious stones of his treasure had to become stones of blood. St John puts the point of change at the feeding of the five thousand when they tried to force Jesus into kingship, a sort of kingship that had nothing to do with the Kingdom of God. Entirely the wrong message had been gained from his presence and preaching. Other Gospel writers put it at the Transfiguration and at the confession of Peter at Caesarea Philippi. They all reinforced his realization that there was only one way forward.

Hidden within his preaching and teaching, hidden within the later parables as positioned by the evangelists, is the knowledge that the treasures of Scripture can only be discovered, uncovered and fulfilled through suffering. There is to be a final trembling. The agonizing classroom of Calvary has become inevitable. As happens with so many people, that living sermon, that living parable, can only strike hearts through disgrace. Whether it is undeserved or deserved probably doesn't matter. Disgrace is one of the chisels God uses to hone those chosen for glory.

> In the Cross of Christ I glory,
> Towering o'er the wrecks of time.
> All the light of sacred story,
> Gathers round that head sublime.

The light of sacred story the preacher or Christian teacher presents through himself can only penetrate minds and hearts through brokenness. Lohengrin's spear was only able to conquer when it had been broken and recast. Stronger and 'conquering' through brokenness. Treasures can only be revealed, pearls can only sparkle when mined from the soil of disgrace, and it doesn't matter whether that disgrace, that brokenness, is, in reality, innocence or fact. As far as the leaders of his day were concerned Jesus was the latter. He was undoubtedly guilty. Such was the crucified Lord and the message from the hill of Calvary. The parable from a broken heart is the most powerful of all and certainly the most exciting treasure in the mind of God's Son.

One other thing before I finally get back to those wonderfully brief parables. The man with the buried treasure, the merchant with the hidden pearl had the knowledge of their presence. The imagining of their hiddenness. They were lying there, waiting for them. And in that knowing is a beauty. The beauty of desire, of potential. Christ had the amazing gift of knowing such presence. He could detect hidden treasures at a hundred yards, whether they dwelt in a leper, a tax collector, or an aged, possible disciple sitting under a tree. He could detect and reveal them with a sensitivity known only to that person. Trampling on hidden treasures was not his practice. Misjudging the value of the ground that hid them was not his style.

At the bottom of the road in which we lived as children was a rather grim-looking house. The single woman who inhabited it was not often seen except on Sundays and early weekday mornings, when she hurried off to church wearing a grey coat and a grey felt hat looking like an inverted pudding basin. After her eucharistic journey she trotted back and disappeared behind her net curtains. Christine, of course, was much younger than we as children thought. Old age began at thirty and infirmity at forty, we considered then. Later her treasure was revealed. She unbeknown to us was the parish pray-er. She rose soon after four in the morning, interceded for three hours, went to church and then returned to her work after a cup of tea. We with many others were included in her prayers. Such were the hidden pearls of her prayerful rosary. Hiddenness as well as realization is part of the great scheme. Hidden in the hill of Calvary are treasures yet undiscovered and enough for the ten thousand future generations of Christians and non-Christians.

The Parables

I have used the two parables as hangers for other thoughts. To get back to my original scheme: they are both loaded with beauty and with risk. The whole telling creates at once a joy of beauty. Scholars can detect in bits of the Gospel words and phrases that are more than likely not genuine, not words of our Lord. They analyse the vocabulary and the style, and the setting of a particular passage. But in many places you do not need your scholarly spectacles. The whole feel is right or wrong. There is a skill, a beauty of expression, a freshness about the genuine that is lacking in the suspect. These two little parables have the overwhelming feel of the master about them. Certainly they too breathe risk. The selling of all to obtain one's heart's desire. And again that desire has the feel of the master's heart about it. Unlike the Jewish version of the story there is an open-endedness about these two little treasures. What they did with the pearl, how they stored or spent the treasure is not described. The joys are endless but not told. The leaving of it unsaid is typical of this lordly story-teller.

Most commentators would agree that in essence both parables make one simple point. It is the joy of discovery. The thrill of possession. Let me quote from Jeremias who has a brilliant paragraph about it all. He says,

> The key words are in Matthew Chapter 13, verse 44, 'because of the joy'. When that great joy, surpassing all measure, seizes a man, it carries him away, penetrates his inmost being, subjugates his mind. All else seems valueless compared with that surpassing worth. No price is too great to pay. The unreserved surrender of what is most valuable becomes a matter of course. The decisive thing in the twin parables is not what the two men give up, but the reason for their doing so, the overwhelming experience of the splendour of their discovery. Thus it is with the Kingdom of God. The effect of the joyful news is overpowering; it fills the heart with gladness; it makes life's whole aim the consummation of the divine community and produces the most whole-hearted self-sacrifice.

A wonderful summary of what the faith is about. Getting the balance between the joy and the self-sacrifice is not in a sense necessary because one follows on naturally from the other. Sacrifice is dissolved into the joy. But Christians are good at separating the two and it usually produces unattractive results. We all know Christians who appear to concentrate, or major as some would term it, completely on the joy. No self-sacrifice seems to have been involved. It is as if the whole life of faith is all sparkling wine and cream cakes. While others give witness to a faith which makes the desert Fathers look cosy. Both characters in the parables see, know, the presence of the treasure first. They see the prize and give their all to obtain it They do not give their all in the vain hope that there is a treasure at the end. There may have been moments when they thought the deal would collapse, that the goal was going to be impossible but it would have been a realized unattainable, and sometimes the joy of the faith is like that also. That realized yet at present unattainable vision controls all that is done, the now, and that which we have in view.

I once knew a very old nun. This nun told me that as a young novice she had been granted an overwhelming knowledge of the presence of God, a grasping of the treasures of the divine. Since then, she said, her prayers, even her sacramental life, her Bible study and offices had been in comparison no more than routine, and at times just drudgery. But the knowledge that she had sensed the pearl of great price had been enough. Vision enough for the journey, however long it was.

The joy of the discovery is the completely unexpected point the parables make (compared with the old version of the story), and the hard work, the self-sacrifice of selling all to obtain it is subsidiary. The hearers would have expected the usual type of ending. The old version of the tale very like the one Jesus told is of a man who inherited a great pile of rubbish. Being a lazy person he didn't search through it and sold it to someone else for a trivial sum. The purchaser, however, sifted through it and found a treasure and used it to build a great palace. When the seller saw him pass through the bazaar with a train of slaves he could have choked himself with annoyance. Christ's ending, the joy simply of attaining the treasure, would have taken the crowd completely by surprise. Total surprise.

And the Cross and Passion are exactly that. 'It was for the joy that was set before him that Christ endured the Cross despising the disgrace.' The Cross is the treasure, the pearl of great price. It is as simple as that, and its costly attainment is in a sense subsidiary. The search for that joy redeems the hunt. Lent is our acting-out of that treasure-hunt. It is the treasures of the Crucified that we are after and if we concentrate on the disciplines on the way it is unlikely that we will arrive at Easter ready for the joy. Honed for the handling of the pearls. However many bits of palm trees or St Veronica's handkerchiefs we pick up on the way there.

And the real excitement is that Lent is in no way an earning exercise. Holy Week and Easter are the reclaiming of the treasure that is already ours. Not an earned treasure or a prize for having made a good job of the forty days but pearls that are already our possession. I probably misunderstand St Paul, as I do not think that it is a case of 'run that you may obtain'. The great and overwhelming joy is that the treasure is already ours. It is there waiting for us. It is already ours. It is not a Sir Francis Drake prayer affair, pursuing the task until it is thoroughly finished. The task has already been completed for us by Christ and we don't need to lift a finger to complete it. Of course doing so because we are joining Christ is a treasure anyway, the joy, but it is his companionship not the sweating it out that counts, and is the wonder on the way. The treasure is there waiting for us, and whatever we do it won't go away. It will always surprise us. It will always be there. The ultimate thesaurus of God.

12

The Unjust Judge

St Luke 18: 1–8

Catechisms are no longer fashionable. Learning the faith, or anything else, by question and answer rote is not thought educationally sound. The days of 'keeping my hands from picking and stealing' are over. Nowadays multiple choice questions seem to be *de rigueur*. Perhaps 'Is the Father incomprehensible, the Son incomprehensible, the Holy Ghost incomprehensible or all three incomprehensible?' Circle one.

Were I to construct a catechism containing questions on prayer, one of the answers to the question, 'What is prayer?' would be: explorations into the nature of God. And certainly one of the sources of prayer, as far as that definition is concerned, would be the parables. Time and time again by a simple story, original, or an old restored and revitalized by the master's paint box, Jesus gives us an insight into the nature of God and hence into the nature of humanity as well. God's liberality of forgiveness; humanity's hardness of heart. God's love of the poor and despised; humanity's rejection of them. The parables highlight the properties of God and by comparison our own, and those divine characteristics can become part of our adoration and thanksgiving and are often by contrast part of our confession. The parable of the Unjust Judge is partly about the widow's persistence, her continual beseechings, and that too should be an element in our prayers.

But it is not only the subject of the parables, persistence etc., that illuminate the features of prayer, it is also the nature of the parables themselves that do so. To use a Sunday School-type method, let me mention four words all beginning with S in this context. First, the parables are wonderfully skilful, and must have taken our Lord enormous time and thought in their construction. Prayer is without doubt a skill, though in some people it seems as natural as breathing. Naturalness, too, is part of the skill of the parables and must have been developed by Jesus, as with his prayer life, by practice. Natural fluency like that of the top tennis player or the concert pianist is developed by hard work.

Prayer also needs working at for its development into the sort of prayer God would have it be. This will mean set times, probably a method, and there are scales and arpeggios to be gone through before one can advance to the sonatas and scherzos of prayer. Even ways of sitting or kneeling for prayer are part of all this. St Teresa of Avila used to say, 'Comfortable but not too comfortable'. She went on to say that at times there was a mere whisker between prayer and sleep! The skill of our Lord's prayer life, as far as we know it, like his parables, seems to be a result of practice and tough keeping at it. Hence about persistence in prayer, and hence the parable of the widow.

The fact that Jesus seems to have been able to produce a parable or a saying for all occasions at will, means that his explorations into the nature of God were continual. They were a state, my second S, a state of mind and heart. He lived in that state of exploration. And in a sense, prayer also should be a continual state of mind and spirit. Of course, as with our Lord, there will be moments or hours of actual prayer, adoration, beseeching, etc. (Luther in a letter to someone wrote, 'I am so busy at the moment that I cannot afford to do less than four hours of prayer a day') but prayer should be the constant background of our being. The backcloth and scenery of the stage on which we lead our lives. The widow's cause may have been the background of her life, but although she was battering the judge with it, it wouldn't have done her cause any good if she had been battering her neighbours with it as well! Prayer is a state of being in the presence of God, but not always conscious of it.

My third S is 'sharing'. The parables are like a reversible chemical reaction. They are earthly tales yet are always reacting with the heavenly and back again, and hence sharing and partaking of both. Intercessory prayer is often a sharing in God's work for his world. Bringing God to his world and his world to God as we do supremely in the offering of the Eucharist. Our depths vibrating with God's depths over matters small and great in his creation. That vibrating of one with the other is exactly the feel the parables have about them. The importunate widow wanted to share her concerns with the unwilling judge. To intercede with him. Intercessory prayer may be the most difficult, theologically, for obvious reasons, but it is also the most natural. If God knows all our desires already why bother to ask him? But bother him we do, and Jesus in this parable makes it clear that we should. Intercessory world tours at the Eucharist often take longer than the sermon!

The last S, though I am sure there are plenty more relevant to prayer, is the word style. The master's mark. And this is often the reason why attachments to the parables can be allotted to another author. The style is wrong. I consider that in prayer it is very important to develop one's own style. One that resonates with the character of the pray-er. It can be wonderful to borrow from the great Christians of prayer: St Bernard, St Francis, Charles Simeon, William Temple, Charles de Foucauld, and so on. But try merely copying them, Bernard on Monday, Francis on Tuesday, John of the Cross on Wednesday, and you will end up with a prayer breakdown on Thursday. Each of us is hand-crafted by God in some way or other, and our style-link with him will be different and part of our divine gifts.

One other thought about prayer before I tackle this tricky little parable. No doubt many of us were taught that the word ACTS in acts of prayer was a mnemonic of prayer itself. A for adoration, C for confession, T for thanksgiving, and S for supplication. Useful perhaps. We were told we should put our adoration of God top of the list, daily make confession of our wrongdoings, and so on. But it is the other way round that gets missed out in our thinking about the parables. We concentrate on the failure of the priest and Levite to cross barriers and on the fact the goodie was a Samaritan, rather than what the parables say about God.

Likewise in prayer. The overwhelming thing is not our often puny adoration of God, but God's adoration, even worship, of us his creation. If imitation is the sincerest form of flattery, how about the fact that God was incarnate in human likeness? That is the extent of his adoration of humankind. Amazing. Likewise confession. When we confess to God and our eiderdown at night we are often telling God either directly or on occasions through a priest some of the essential, if unpleasant bits of our nature. We are saying this is what we are like. This is what makes us tick. Likewise, Christ is God's confession to us. Goodness beyond compare in this case. In Christ, God is saying this is what I am like. This is what makes me tick. And part of God's confession to us is seen in the nature of the parables.

Likewise, thanksgiving and supplication should be seen God-wise rather than always human-wise. We are in a sense, as is all creation, God's thanksgiving for himself, and particularly sharingly so in Christ. In Christ, God supplicates, beseeches us, to be as he is. Supremely this ACTS of prayer from God reaches its climax in the lived-out parable of the Cross, and reaches its finale in the reality of parable: the resurrection.

There are those who tell me that we must start where 'they' are. 'They', presumably, being other mortals who haven't their insights. Obviously starting with high-flown theology is probably not advisable, but I have always found that people have stores of 'natural' theology, well thought-out, that need tapping. I am also told that our courses, etc., must be relevant. Perhaps, perhaps. But preaching and teaching must also start with an insight into the burning mysteries, love and purposes of the Holy Trinity. The undiluted God is more relevant than anything else to our lives. He is where we are continually, even if veiled from our sight. So you might as well start where *he* is, and the parables are, therefore, a good place to start that prayerful, teaching, preaching exploration into the nature of God.

The Parable

Despite its apparent shortness and straightforwardness the parable has some complex characteristics in language and construction. For instance the words, 'I will give her justice before she wears me out.' The word translated 'wears me out' literally means 'hits me under the eye'. Some translators prefer to use the phrase 'before she deafens me', which is probably more correct, but seems an odd anatomical switch. There are oddities, too, with sudden changes in syntax and mood which makes one wonder what the original telling sounded like. But whatever the difficulties it is wonderfully startling parable. Amazing that our Lord should use the story of a brutal and insensitive judge to illustrate God's help to those who pray persistently. Judge Jeffreys was not, I suspect, a person used to illustrate the nature of God from late seventeenth-century pulpits. Such usage must have startled and scandalized Jesus's hearers and so in this case the story could not be left without some interpretation. Hence the addition of verses 6–8 which in this case are usually thought to be by our Lord.

It is closely connected with the parable in Luke 11, verses 5–8 about a man woken in the night. He is already in bed, on the rug on the floor under the blanket with his family, when he is asked for help. A complicated business to get up to attend to the caller's needs. But the parable makes the same point as that of the Judge. If a human being, and in the first case a bad-tempered one, in the end listens to the needy, how much more so will the ever-loving and ever-listening Father. It is an argument that Jesus loves using. If human beings, sinful as they are, show kindness to their children and to others, how much more so will God do likewise. If humanity makes sacrificial gifts to their offspring how much more will the Almighty give sacrificially. The shadow of the Cross is in all such *a fortiori* arguments.

As we know from examples in the Old Testament, widows and orphans typified those who were helpless, defenceless and usually poor. As we also know from the history books of Samuel and Kings, getting justice was an almost impossible process for those who had no money to bribe the judges. Jesus is once more heightening the difficulty of poverty and the power and scandal of riches and using that predicament to show that we should keep on praying and never lose heart.

But, strangely enough, the Old Testament is also full of those who long for the courts, for justice. Divine justice in the courts of heaven, as well as earthly justice. 'Give sentence with me, O God, and defend my cause against the ungodly people', pleads the psalmist. Job knew that his vindicator lived, and that he would rise at last to speak for him in court. The now penniless Job longed to justify his innocence in the courts of God. The deprived poor longed for life to be just, to be in court so that they could justify themselves. We are not without examples of such in modern life. In Israel God's justice was seen not only as the punishment of the wicked, but above all as the vindication of those who were battered by life and the system. Again the *a fortiori* argument applies. If this widow actually gets what she desperately desires in the form of her rightful deserts from such a judge, how much more will all the underdogs, the helpless and destitute finally get what they long for when God comes with judgement. In this sense the ordinary people didn't dread the justice of God, Judgement Day, the justice of the Messiah; they longed for it. They would get their rights and their enemies their come-uppance.

And it has to be asked, what difference does the Cross make to all this? What does the injustice of Calvary do for the forwarding of justice, for the injustice suffered by the despised? It cannot be surely a rather superficial, 'It will all come right in the end. Don't worry, despite all this resurrection is on the way'. 'Bear your injustice patiently because God will vindicate you in the life to come.' Clearly there is something in those comforts and the Church has felt justified in preaching them down the ages. There is also the joyful comfort affirmed by so many of the martyrs that they were sharing in the disgrace and sufferings of Christ; that they were advancing the coming of God's Kingdom of righteousness, by parading the spectacle, the triumphal procession of Christ's Passion. But shared injustice doesn't remove the injustice or lessen it in any way, even if it does advertise it.

I suspect there are no answers to the problem as such. Freewill will always mean that injustice is a possibility. Just as the nature of God will always mean that in Christ's Passion he involves himself in the tragedy and in the pain of the process of injustice. The longing of the widow. And God follows through with his involvement in the results of that injustice. But he will no more rescue humanity from that injustice than he did his Son, except in the advertisement of love involved, seen in the injustice of the Cross and Passion. That silent billboard is the only powerless pressure he is prepared to exercise on the hearts of those who peddle such injustices. But we have little idea what the justice of God will be, except that it will be swamped with mercy for both plaintiff and defendant. Neither, as an afterthought, do we know, I suspect, the nature of what God in the end calls sinful, or what is responsibly sinful. We may well be rushing between the dock and every other part of the court on Judgement Day!

A couple of postscripts to this mysterious parable. First, so many of the parables are set amidst the ordinary affairs of ordinary people. The two I have mentioned in this chapter, that of the Unjust Judge and the householder disturbed at midnight must have been not uncommon occurrences in first century Palestine. They are stories which many of Jesus's hearers would have been involved in themselves in some way. The parables are the jewels of Christ's skill of merging the heart of the nature of God with mankind's ordinariness. From the first word of the story his encapsulation of the familiar by the nature of God begins, whether the ordinary be frustration, as it is in this parable, a woman doing her daily chores, or a shepherd in search of a lost sheep. It is this encapsulation that opens the minds of Jesus's hearers and still has the power to do so today.

Secondly, there is that equally mysterious last verse: 'When the Son of Man comes, will he find faith on earth?' Is this verse an encouragement to his close followers to whom it seems to be addressed rather than to the crowds? It is a chapter full of the difficulties of discipleship, and here is a challenge to be trusting despite what is to come. Preparation of his disciples for their future roles is well on the way and here is an encouragement to persistence in prayer and faith which will be sorely needed in the times ahead. But it hangs in the air like so many of the verses that follow parables and has its effect by so doing. To be taken away for future use which is part of a disciple's preparation anyway.

13

The Labourers in the Vineyard

St Matthew 20: 1–16

A wartime childhood was not an extravagant affair. Cholesterol levels may have been low, a pat or two of butter a week and an egg if you were lucky. Bath levels were low too. Five inches and no more. No extravagances. No lashing out with food, drink, light or fuel, and I suspect it all had a lasting effect on many of us. Thickly-spread butter became almost impossible, ever after. Cream cakes considered border-line sin. The iron of meanness entered into our souls and was difficult to rust away. Generosity became a thought-out affair, seldom impulsive. Extravagance, an indulgence to be restrained.

Whether the good Lord came from a poor or vaguely 'middle class' background is a tricky assessment. Monastics distinguish between the poverty of Bethlehem, the poverty of Nazareth, and the poverty of Calvary, and have at times discussed those states extrava-gantly. But whichever it was, with a greedy occupying power demanding taxes to finance the army and an army of legislators, and with the Temple tax claiming yet more, the ordinary family was not killing fatted calves daily. Jesus's home was probably poor but not poverty-stricken. Simple, but not deprived. Extravagance, a once-a-year affair. A celebration on a feast or two.

Yet, unlike our wartime souls (and many Jews would have con-sidered themselves in a perpetual state of war against the occupying power), Jesus adores extravagance. He revelled in outrageous generos-ity. A puritanical face at the thought of a party was not his, and he didn't seem to mind who threw it and where. On page after page of the Gospels his love of extravagance and unbridled generosity comes through. Forty days of fasting in the wilderness seems to have been a preparation for a perpetual outpouring. Just as the utter poverty of

Calvary was a preparation for the extravagance of Easter. And in his ministry Jesus extends this extravagance into the theological ideas of his ministry. The parables are full of it.

He is certainly fond of extravagance with food and drink. A hundred and twenty-seven gallons of wine, in the jars holding two or three firkins apiece, acording to St John, was enough for a drunken village. Though that is not the point the evangelist is making. Why does the Good News Bible, whose illustrations I admire, translate the word in the story as 'miracle', when it plainly in this context means 'sign'? 'This beginning of *signs* did Jesus', not beginning of *miracles*. A sign means pointing to the future or to someone, in this case, Jesus. A miracle points to the act. The creation of a superior wine. It is important to distinguish between the two. The changing of the water points to the nature of Jesus, what he is, what he has come for. He is not primarily a miracle-worker. He is a sign. He is a sign of sparkling extravagant life.

There is another sign, too, a few chapters on in St John's Gospel and repeated in all the Gospels, the sign of the feeding of the five thousand. Again, there is incredible extravagance, inspired generosity, with enough food left over to feed another sitting. It is almost uncontrolled extravagance. Out-of-hand generosity.

On another occasion, Zacchaeus, tax gatherer of little stature, when he had been noticed by Jesus and collected into his friendship, threw a party for his newly-found charismatic wandering Rabbi. Many of the parables are feasting ones. In much ancient culture one of the joys of the afterlife was the heavenly banquet. And Jesus loved it too.

Extravagance is an interesting word. It was an epithet of certain Papal decrees not contained in particular collections. In other words, they were documents not found in the normal piles of this and that. They were outside the bounds of the ordinary, the normal. Literally, something that wandered outside the normal. And the parables are time and time again extravagant in that sense. They not only tell stories of happenings where there is a twist or two, that go beyond the normal, they are designed to force us to push our thinking beyond the bounds of normality too. That is their exploration into the nature of God. A God who has to be seen and recognized beyond the boundaries of normal doctrine, beyond the limits of ordinary thinking as well as within them.

This parable certainly does that, as we shall see. The parable on Forgiveness goes into an extravagant stratosphere. Clearly the parables of the Prodigal Son and the Good Samaritan do also. Crossing the road boundary, going outside the rival nationality boundary. They are extravagant stories going way outside the normal theological thinking of the nature of God as far as the Jewish rulers were concerned. They are very often father stories, too, or father-like ruler stories. One of a father giving a banquet for his son. This one of a father-like landowner and employer. The Prodigal's father and so on.

Jesus, as Michael Ramsey constantly used to point out, points to his Father not to himself in what he does and says, only rarely to himself. Jesus wishes to push out, to enlarge thinking on the issues of the day, both religious and secular. Issues such as healing, when and where; chosen-nation status, as opposed to the outsider; forgiveness and its authority and limits; riches and whether they were a blessing or a danger. We could make a similar list for today's issues without much trouble, I suspect.

To return. Food and drink extravagance, yes, but the tougher generosity, the ultimate outpouring is with himself. Time, concern, compassion, prayer, emotions, every sort of personal energy are given without sparing or stinting. From early morning onwards nothing was allowed to get in the way. Total self-giving, personal extravagance given without limit. Even as a boy in the Temple at Jerusalem there seems to have been an extremity of questioning. He grilled the Rabbis. Wonderful and infuriating. Stretching from the call of the disciples to the Cross there is a totality about it all. A directed and planned generosity as well as an impulsive one. The Kingdom of Heaven was at hand and it couldn't wait. Men and women had to be healed whether it were the Sabbath or not. The extravagance of the *now*. We get the feeling of an exhausting pace about so much of the Gospels. A burning desire to get to Jerusalem for the final outpouring of himself. For the Cross and Passion. There is a wonderful passage where the writer says he went before them up to Jerusalem. Ahead, with a determination which nothing would stop. The total generosity of heart and soul, of life and limb. The extravagant claim of Kingship acted out in the entry to the city. The terrible wrath with the money-changers. The incredible claim that the bread and wine at the Last Supper are his body and blood. The whole drama to the end is extreme in every way. Even the skies respond with totality. Total blackness. It is love unbounded. Extravagance is a theme of parable and Passion.

This unlimited generosity, this unbounded love is not just directed at friends or the like-minded and especially so in the Passion, where there is a feeling of embracing all. Throughout Christ's ministry no one is barred from this extravagance of charisma. Tax collectors, prostitutes (if they were such), lepers, babes and aged, all and sundry and mostly the sundry are included. Gifts are poured out from beginning to end of his ministry without distinction, the final extravagance being the gift of paradise to the penitent thief. James in his Epistle has a delightful passage about not making distinctions with generosity, so clearly it wasn't many years into the Church before gifts and status and love had some tests attached to them.

Just one and a half other points before I tackle the parable. Jesus expected his disciples to be and do likewise in their outpouring. He finds meanness by anyone despicable. He would not have admired some of our restraint gained from wartime. He expects his followers to be completely generous without distinction. He rebukes them when they question such things. The five thousand will be fed whatever the practical difficulty the disciples put in the way. Meanness should not be on the Christian menu either from individuls or organizations. Children must be brought to him. The Kingdom of God required it, whether the disciples thought so or not. He rebukes his host at a party for the meanness of his welcome compared with the welcome he gets from a woman of doubtful morals. The parable of Forgiveness is also about the meanness of the debtor compared with the generosity of the king.

I realize that the institution of the Eucharist was a 'private' affair, a family affair, a farewell affair with the disciples. In other words, the partakers of the bread and wine were limited by discipleship, but I would contend that the sealing of that meal, its completion as a Eucharist is the crucifixion. 'Sealed in my blood' and 'until I drink it afresh' find their fulfilment in the Kingdom of Heaven. Mysterious phrases that seem to open it up and the Cross where it was sealed was a public affair in every way. The institution of such grace may have been private but its sealing and proclamation couldn't have been more public. The Cross broadcasts grace to all people, all of which is worth a hammer and tongs discussion or three.

And the half point is this. Jesus also despised pseudo-extravagance. The Pharisees who threw their money around in a public way but could have given much more, compared unfavourably with the widow and her mites which exhausted her current account. Pseudo-extravagance paraded extravagantly compared with the giving that hurts. Lent may be a time to give up luxuries, but not if that blinds us to generous giving. Ask many of the charities where tear-producing contributions come from when disasters happen.

The Parable

And now to the parable itself, which I love. I have never been to the Holy Land and stood in a village market-place, so I can't picture the scene accurately. Men standing in the sun for a while, then perhaps in the shade of a fig tree, waiting for someone to employ them. The risk of the casual labourer is humiliating and depressing, however beautiful the scene may be. How is the family to be clothed and fed? Both of almost equal importance to the Jew. All a risky business. We need to feel the power of the scene. Be in the picture, be characters in the drama. Particularly that last scene with the labourers lined up to receive their wages. Then comes the bombshell of equal pay and the grumbles about sweating in the heat of the day. What's it all about?

There is a fascination about the way that different scholars interpret the parables. C. H. Dodd sees them all in terms of the last things, eschatology. In terms of judgement. Jeremias, more varied but quite different, and so on with other scholars, men and women. Is this a parable about Jesus's ministry to the despised, as some would have us believe? 'The first shall be last and the last first?' A *logion* that occurs immediately before the parable as well as after it. The saying surrounds the parable which occurs after Jesus has been listing the rewards the disciples can expect in the Kingdom of Heaven. Christ was forever making it clear that the poor and lowly, the outsiders, were first through the gates of heaven. Those who were probably not synagogue worshippers or considered good keepers of the commandments. Is the parable about those despised outsiders who seem to have been most sensitive to the generosity of his preaching? Not the insiders who though they may have sweated on had the thickest net curtains to their lives?

Is it concerned with the nature of the reward and everyone gets the same pay in the end, which I suppose on strictly logical thinking must be so? Heaven is heaven and there can't be some parts of it that are more heavenly than other parts. Seeing God is total fulness and can't be anything less. And all this despite what we like to think about those whose faith we are not quite sure is full-blooded. Generosity without distinction must be one of the joys of heaven. Just as the benefits of Christ's Passion are open to all without distinction and, I like to think, without distinction of different faiths.

The main point I want to make (the parable may or may not make it), and which I think is central to its meaning and a lot else, is: can we in any way earn our way into heaven? Is heaven a prize for the winner of the race as St Paul seems to imply? If there is no 'advantage' in being good, in worshipping, in noble works, and everyone is finally in for ambrosia, why bother with such things, which are often an effort and go against the grain? There is no doubt that most of us consider that those of us who have been moral believers, loving believers, deserve the front seats in the heavenly Kingdom. We are certain God is fair. We earn our way in. We think it must be so, either by faith or good works.

Such matters are, of course, beyond our comprehension, though I confess to being a universalist. Certainly the answers are hidden in the Cross and Passion, for it is in a sense an act that has both total and no-earning value. Christ 'does' nothing in his Passion. It is all done *to* him. But in its happening it achieves the salvation of the world, past, present and future, and that salvation is totally inclusive. Waiting, hoping, in that market-place, whatever the reason, and whatever they did as they waited, was a work. We do not know why or what causes people not to be 'earners' in the way we think they should be and we have no right to judge. 'Waiting, being passive, is a great work.'

The main realization is, of course, that working for God, worshipping God is its own reward. We need no more, whether it is here or after death. The Kingdom of God is already come. So there is no need to envy the pennies of the latecomers. We are only thankful that they have joined the working band. They who started on their joyful labours early cannot laud it over those who started late. Extravagant generosity shown by the landowner should be the happiness of the early birds as well as the late ones. He knows more about the hearts and souls of all the labourers than we do.

14

The Pharisee and the Publican

St Luke 18: 9–14

In Palestine in the time of our Lord, publicans, tax men, were syn-onymous with cheats and frauds, extracting more than their due from the poor and vulnerable and keeping the change. Traitorous collabor-ators with the occupying power. If there had been a pantomime-type audience listening to Jesus when he told this short parable, a beauti-fully crafted one, there would have been hissing when the Publican was mentioned and polite coughing perhaps when the Pharisee was introduced. A respected group, some of them without doubt holy men, but not the religious pop stars of the ancient world.

Jesus in the parables constantly turns the accepted thinking, the ordinary likes and dislikes, upside down. Both in these wonderful situation stories and in the actual encounters with people in the Gospels. Christ makes his central character, in story or reality, some-one from a despised, rejected, sin-living, or hated group. A publican, a Samaritan, a leper, a poor man. He goes out of his way to down the respectable and up the unloved. Perhaps the point Jesus is making, and this parable is a glorious illustration of such thinking, is the sensitivity and potential of the hurt. If I had to list the characteristics of our Lord that 'force' me to believe he was God incarnate, that make me bow the knee to him, I would put this gift of seeing the inner nature of men and women near the top of my list. As St John remarks at the beginning of his Gospel: 'because he knew what was in man'. Often down history it has been the hurt and rejected who have been the most sensitive in art and music. They have explored the depths through their hurt and turned it into beauty.

Time and time again, without playing down the fact that some of the characters in his parables were sinners, had offended, Jesus sees behind the hardness, the brashness, to the person within, to the adult wonderful creation aching to climb out of the chrysalis, or, sometimes, to the glory within unknown and unrealized even by the characters themselves. Sinners often make better saints than those who have never trespassed with vigour.

I cannot over-emphasize how much I consider this a priority job of the Church. Exploring the sensitivity of the hurt, who of necessity often have put on their concrete case, and releasing the potential within. Having worked as a schoolmaster and a university chaplain, I know this to be so, and grace is the power that releases human beings from themselves. And of course this applies both to communities and to individuals. Grace in the word of parable and in the sacrament of parable, which contain the nature of God hidden within story, does its work. I have seen hundreds of children and students who have never been treated sensitively in word or deed, have never had beautiful sounds or shapes around them, have never been listened to at depth, and have been abused with false ideas of adulthood and how to treat others. Gradually over the years the concrete has gone on, and it requires the moving, penetrating power-drill of parable to reveal the true self within. Somewhere hidden in this parable is a power of that kind.

The living parable of the Cross is the most powerful, the most sensitive drill of all, because our Lord not only identifies with the concrete covering of humanity but by so doing redeems it. If we take the text of the Passion at its face value, Christ penetrates the steel façade of Pilate, if only for a moment. He gets through the coating of the penitent thief and, in one translation of the text anyway, he opens the sealed eyes of the centurion in charge of the crucifixion who witnesses Jesus's death. But, but, he cannot get through to the men of religious power; for the concrete of religious power is the thickest, the most reinforced of all, the Gospels seem to imply.

By identifying with the hurt and desensitized as he moves through the Gospels, and particularly in the Passion, Jesus awakens and reveals the real person within. But he fails to open the inner eye of the men of power and respect. All of which is a lengthy diversion from where I began with the parable, yet a terrifying picture of how Christ often finds criminals, the immoral, the rejected and despised, the hardened and the unholy, the Publican for instance, easier nuts to crack than the powerful, and particularly the servants of God with functional authority.

The Parable

To the parable itself. It is beautiful. It is a miniature, a glorious *Missa Brevis*. There is a rather complex-sounding statement by the painter Degas. He said, 'I don't paint so that people can see what I paint, but in order that they may see what *I* see when I paint'. Jesus wants us to see what he sees when he paints these parables. Not what a superficial observer might see. Comparison within the picture is often the essence of good art. Contrast both in colour and subject. Here it is starkly so, as it is with the Good Samaritan, though perhaps this parable's closest neighbour is the Prodigal with the comparison of the two sons. The righteous older one and the good-for-nothing younger one.

I do not think that primarily we have a comparison between hypocrisy and humility, even though the little phrase at the end may imply so, with one of the characters anyway. That particular aphorism occurs in one form or other in several parts of the Gospel. I like to think that the Gospel writers had a bundle of sayings that may have been said by Jesus and stuck them into the Gospel when they found a place where they vaguely fitted. What I do think Jesus is doing is declaring that our virtues can cut us off from God almost more finally that our sins can. The Pharisee had religious virtue and there was no doubt about that. The list of his fulfilments of the law, what he believed God required, was certainly virtuous according to Jewish thought. He lined himself up with the ten commandments and being the man he was he would have pondered the law day and night. 'Thy word is a lantern unto my feet, and a light unto my paths.' There was nothing wrong in being grateful to God that he wasn't like some other men. But these virtues had cut him off from other people and hence from God.

One of our Lenten exercises should be to look not only at our vices but also to take a thorough look at what we suspect are our virtues (and most of us are quite clear about them) and particularly our religious ones. I go to church three times a week, I give to five charities, I sometimes visit the sick, and I cook Sunday lunch for my grandchildren. There is a wonderful parody of such thinking in Auberon Waugh's *Foxglove Saga*. How far in fact do these things and others unite us more closely to God and to our neighbour and do we care if they do as long as we have fulfilled our observances? Isolated virtue and cold charity are more terrifying often than greed and adultery (which the Pharisee lists).

One other thing. The danger with virtue is that it can make you over-confident. There is a motto (in Latin, for disguise and respectability) which states 'By strength and by virtue'. Terrifying. One of them is enough to isolate you from the weak, frightened sinner. Two can lead to a Lazarus – Dives distance. All of us in our jobs have met that confidence that stamps on the sensitivity of the nervous. Not wittingly, but just because the shutters of confidence have come down over the windows of empathy. Confidence without large penetrable joints in its armour leads to Pharisaism.

Virtue's blindness seems to have been one of the things that our Lord found most hard to bear. There is, for instance, an arrogant confidence, claimed as virtue, in those who 'know' they are right about the content of their faith. They seem to claim that they have Jesus wrapped up and they are happily wrapped up in him. They have definite answers to this and that, mostly gleaned from one sort of interpretation of Scripture. That sort of confidence, that sort of 'we are not as other men are', is a cul-de-sac or a circular road, without the hesitancy of exploration and without the glory of the possibility of change.

Paul is quite clear that when we are weak then are we strong. Failure and weakness are central to the Gospel and found mostly in the outcast, and so-called sinners, perhaps. Of course such things can lead to bitterness and despair. The confidence of success, however, and the total lack of hesitancy at times of the successful, can be almost impenetrable. Hence Jesus's forthrightness against the specimen of religious success in this parable, and his award of God's accolade of justification to the Publican.

The Cross is failure's gracefulness. The benefits of Christ's Passion are open especially, it would seem, to the broken, the failed, and his disciples were the first to have such life-giving grace poured upon them. Could they have received it without the brokenness of their treachery, I wonder? I do not like the word 'power' in most contexts, but the strength of total weakness is the power of the Cross. The compassion of failure is central to our crucified faith and to this parable.

To end with a few remarks based on my three primary characteristics. There is a beauty of vulnerability in the Publican. The beauty of remorse, the beauty of standing in the background, yet being in the spotlight of Christ's attention, compared with the ugliness of over-confident virtue. Such a comparison is often achieved in the biblical

paintings of great artists. This is also a risky parable. This is characteristic of so many parables. He exposes the concrete-heartedness of the
rich (Lazarus and Dives), the Temple rulers (the Good Samaritan),
and the Pharisees here. He seals his fate through parable. It is open-
ended again in the sense of 'take it away and make what you will of it
for yourself'. Those that have ears to hear then hear.

Here we have a simple story of contrast but it has an incredibly
moving poignancy. Like all parables it is a look-in-the-mirror story,
but here the mirror should lead to further work with a magnifying
glass.

15

The Last Supper as Parable

St Mark 14: 17–26

The 'High Mass' of the Sunday lunch with its attendant rituals, and the 'Holy Communion' of the evening meal with its fewer rites are on the way out in many families, I gather. A quick grab from the fridge, a swift liaison with the microwave and the family members go to the television or the computer. Your companion is the screen in the bedroom and your friends are found by machinery. I exaggerate, perhaps, but the concept of the family, of friends and neighbours, is changing. There are other forms of kinship and closeness. Contact is achieved in other ways.

I wonder, however, whether certain rituals often akin to those of the Eucharist meal will suffer. The liturgy of eating and all that goes with it will be lost. In my youth the Sunday lunch proceeded by the demands of unwritten rubrics, a changing out of scruffiness into comparatively tidy vestments, a hand-washing as did priests of old, was a relaxed yet formal affair. Without the children realizing it, or our parents knowing they were doing so perhaps, wisdom and family traditions were imparted. It was a time of what I believe is now called bonding, achieved by humour, shared enjoyment, quarrels, tears of laughter or temper, which eventually led to renewed closeness.

There was a rehearsal of the past: 'What have you been doing this morning dear?' 'Was it a good week at school or at the office?'; and a looking forward to the future: 'What are you thinking of doing this afternoon?' Even a discussion of what the more distant future might hold. Local, national or international were thrown in and a teasing about relationships. Certainly, though indefinable, there was a family presence, different yet in many ways similar for every family, as I realized when I had the privilege of Sunday lunch in vicarages. And there were rituals, too, of leaving the dining room, with voices of thanksgiving, or in our younger days permission to get down. (I remember a small child at the communion rail after I had blessed him asking his mother if he could get down.) *Ita missa est.* Such meals had the characteristics of liturgy hidden within them. Are such formalities, such liturgies, even in worship, in danger of being lost and does it matter if they are anyway? I suspect it does, as they answer to something very deep in us, both in the home and in worship.

And I need hardly say that the Bible and the Gospels in particular are loaded with meals. The Bible begins with loss of freedom through eating in a garden. It ends with freedom to eat from the tree of life (Revelation 22:14). Paradise lost and regained through eating. St John in his Gospel after an introductory chapter begins Christ's ministry with a wedding, though there comes a point when it may become a dangerously dry one. The sign of new sparkling life takes over at his hands. And John's Gospel ends with breakfast on the sea-shore, when he sends out his disciples with their job instructions having redeemed them.

Luke ends with more than a hint of the Eucharist at Emmaus. The knowing of Christ through the breaking of bread. In the body of the Gospels Jesus is accused of being a glutton and a wine-bibber. Meals pop up all over the place, with our Lord eating in the company of sinners, with the supposedly righteous, on a grassy slope at the feeding of the 5000, where they sit down in rows like a cabbage plot in a garden! There is that heart-rending party at the end of the parable of the Prodigal Son which the elder brother refuses to join. Hidden in occasions of eating from Cana to Emmaus, in Jesus's meals with Zacchaeus, Levi and others, we can feel the powerful presence of Christ and the presence of redemption. The Eucharist and the nature of its meaning are there.

So a description of the Last Supper as it might have happened falls into place with what I have said. For disguised in the meals of the Gospel, in our ordinary meals, in the meal of meals – the Last Supper and its modern equivalents – are the common happenings, the common rituals, reflecting and portraying the needs of family and community. Reflecting the 'history' of those groups, the anticipation of their future, and a mysterious focusing of presence. No wonder Jesus took enormous trouble to make certain the arrangements for that meal were carefully made. There is a meticulous planning about place and privacy. Nothing must go wrong. It had to be exactly right. The drama had to have the correct scenery and setting.

The Last Supper

Reconstructing the Passover scene can be done, scholars assure us, with reasonable accuracy. The meal began outside the main room where the first of four cups of wine were consumed with solemnity. God was blessed as provider of grape and light. Herbs were then eaten, followed by sweetness in the form of squashed fruits. Then came the presentation of the table of food, a low table, and more wine was prepared and Psalm 113 was sung. One of the first group of Hallel psalms. Hallel meaning praise, because all these psalms begin or end with the words 'Praise the Lord'. This group was often called the Egyptian Hallel to distinguish them from the other Hallel psalms, 146–150. So the wonderful feel of being about to flee out of Egypt in the secret of the night was produced. The trembling of prisoners about to be released.

Then came the main meal of lamb, eaten with bitter herbs and blessed by the man who hosted the occasion. And either during or after the meal came the *Haggadah*, the liturgy of the meal. Originally it seems it was an extempore affair, but it eventually became a formalized ritual stimulated by the asking of questions. Some modern feasts have a similar formality which takes the form of a catechism. Such asking in the *Haggadah* stimulated excitement, the knowing of what is coming, but listening to the story as if it were actually happening. In this case the questions were asked by a younger member about the objects and nature of the feast. Questions children so often ask. 'What does this mean Daddy – Abba?' Not long after this last supper the Son would be asking his Father beseeching questions on the Mount of Olives.

Then came another grace and blessing over a third cup of wine and the meal ended with the intoning of the other Egyptian Hallel psalms, 114–118, over a fourth cup of wine. Psalm 114 with the poignant line 'When Israel came out of Egypt and the house of Jacob from among the strange people'. The drama of the key event in their history, the beginning of freedom was acted out. The past, a 'dead' event of history had become living worship. Past deliverance was lived out in thanksgiving. Final deliverance from oppression of all kinds was looked forward to. Past, present and future were merged and celebrated in blessing and praise. Past, present and future were made real through eating and drinking.

And other characteristics of parable are also present, as always when Jesus is acting and speaking. In this supper we are in the midst of that parable characteristic the sea-shore, between actuality and mystery. We are involved, as also in parable, with the ordinary, bread and wine and the familiar story of the Passover, to which Jesus gives a new twist in the eucharistic formula. Even the little word 'this' taken from the *Haggadah* question 'What is this?', is given a new twist in the eucharistic formula, 'This is my Body.' It is made terrifyingly personal. The final parable of the Cross has begun and will be used as the centre of the forthcoming worship for his Church. It is the saddest yet most exciting feast that history records.

We should feel at the Eucharist that we are actually with the disciples in the Upper Room for Passover. We nowadays have little real understanding of the power of memory, the reality of remembrance, as they did. The calling up of the past was so strong that those families, those groups, celebrating Passover were there, they were part of the flight from Egypt, not just acting it out but there. Not imagining the faces of those pilgrims but seeing the faces of those pilgrims in their faces. Memory became a partaking. Memory was presence. There was reality in the remembering. So it should be with us.

16

The Washing of the Feet as Parable

St John 13: 1–30

If drama is to be good, if it is to move us, it must have a feel of artificiality, an unreality, an abnormality about it. Words and actions must be larger than the ordinary, plots must be contrived, and all done so skilfully that drama doesn't turn into melodrama. St John is a very skilled contriver.

But I demand more. I demand that the characters have that dichotomy of reality and unreality too. They must be tangible, yet also intangible. I must be able to relate to them as closely as to myself, see myself in them, yet I ask at the same time that they have a distance about them. I require that the plot enthrals and captures me almost without my knowing it. A capturing that is voluntary yet irresistible. I am on the stage, I take part, yet at the same time I am in the wings. The drama must speak to me directly, and questioningly, leaving me with a basketful of thoughts and messages. I must take home through the dark night more puzzles than I came with through the lighted streets. I am for a while anyway a different person than when I arrived.

And I ask yet more. I wish to feel the freedom of the actors, yet know there is a direction and director behind it all. Often I wish to be elated yet humbled at the same time, have my emotions changed yet also be 'comforted' in the Christian sense of that word. Light and darkness, humour and *gravitas*, *presto* and *largo*, are contrasts that give penetrating reality to the unreality. Drama may not be about the humdrum, but it affects our ordinariness and gives it meaning. No wonder the original meaning of the word 'drama' was an action, office or duty that one fulfilled.

Without doubt the writer of St John's Gospel is the greatest
dramatist in the New Testament. He may not be everybody's favour-
ite gospeller but he is certainly the Sophocles and Shakespeare
amongst them.

And here we come to Act V in the divine drama. Let me stick to
scene I, the dramatic parable of the Foot Washing, before St John
gives us soliloquy scenes in Chapters 14, 15 and 16. Every criteria for
my drama and more besides are fulfilled. The chapter even begins
with what reads like stage directions. An upper room where supper is
taking place. In the place of honour (probably) as treasurer on Jesus's
left, Judas. John, the beloved disciple, on his right. Jesus rises from the
table and takes off his outer garment. Perhaps the seamless robe
signifying the unity of his humanity and divinity which will not
be divided even later at the crucifixion. The scene is set for scene I,
part I.

As the drama takes place before our eyes, and still does, we feel the
almost studied unreality of it all, which as I have suggested heightens
the reality. It is a real situation. Guests would have had their feet
washed and hardly noticed the servant that did it. The washer would
not have been the lord of the household, let alone the Lord of the
universe, as John's readers will now know. There is an exaggeration of
action and word as Jesus removes his clothes, a heightened tension as
he binds himself with the towel of service. Done with the skill of a
master of the stage. The over-the-top explosion of Peter's words both
before and after Jesus washes the feet of that impulsive giant is pure
drama too. The return to the table, all done with slow effectiveness,
and the explanation of the act intensified by the fact that we know
from Luke's Gospel that the disciples had been bickering about
precedence.

And here comes another of my demands in drama, for behind
Jesus's words about, if he as their master and Lord washes their feet
they ought to wash one another's feet, are a thousand and one other
messages. The message that accepting service from your fellow
human beings is an act of humility, for hidden in them all is the Lord
himself. The reverse message, too, that only giving service and never
being ready to receive it is a form of domination. The message that
we cannot be servants until we allow the Lord to serve us. The
message that we cannot love and forgive others until we allow God to
love and forgive us. The message that we cannot reveal our
'unclothed' selves to Christ, until we allow ourselves to view our

'naked' Lord. In other words until we put no barriers between him and us.

So the scene returns to the table. Jesus and his disciples reclining at it on their left elbows so that they can eat and drink with right hands. A scene of feasting but a scene of dis-ease. Then with a suddenness that is the characteristic of the Johannine Gospel it turns to betrayal. The most uniting of all Jewish 'liturgies', the Passover meal, the most symbolic event in all Hebrew history, the supper which eventually led to new life in the Promised Land under the leadership of Moses, will bring death to a greater than Moses. And there in the midst to bring about that death is a traitor. Again John's audience will know who it is, but the actors, the disciples, do not. Then the in-with-both-feet Peter signals John (you can see the stage directions in the text) and tells him to question Jesus. John whose head would have been but an inch or two from Jesus's chest whispers the question, 'Who is it?'

And it is here perhaps that the characters, other than Christ, somehow disappear into a mist of guilt. For although the labelling morsel, the choice morsel, is given to Judas Iscariot, there is more than a feeling, in all probability a reality, that morsels were given to all. No wonder there is that wonderful chorus in Bach's *St Matthew Passion* where the disciples sing 'Is it I?' For they too will betray their Lord but a few hours later. And it is all written in such a way that the audience too are dragged into the question and answer. No wonder Jesus agonizes in spirit, for here are his chosen friends, and although one of them is chief betrayer, he knows he can trust none of them, and John's readers again know it too. Not only that John was writing at a time when early persecutions had probably begun and the lines of the psalmist 'Yea even mine own familiar friend whom I trusted, who did also eat of my bread, hath laid great wait for me', were being fulfilled, as they were on that fatal night.

There is a story of a holy bishop of Salisbury who at a confirmation, a packed confirmation, got up into the pulpit and quoted a text from John, Chapter 15. Two scenes on from the scene we are thinking about. The words of Jesus to his disciples, 'I no longer call you servants but friends.' Slowly the bishop repeated his text and then with tears in his eyes quoted the words once more. 'Amazing, amazing', said the bishop and got down from the pulpit. He could say no more. The maker and master of all, the Lord whom angels dare not look upon, calls his servants friends and within a few hours they will betray him. John's audience knows it and the honest ones among them will squirm in their theatre seats. No wonder Jesus, whose body is the Church, was troubled in spirit.

And so the morsel is accepted by Judas, the chosen morsel. The stage directions will have made it clear that the leading actor does so with gentle care and with a look of compelling love. He gives the betrayer every chance to think again. He has trusted him as treasurer of the apostolic band. He has put him in the place of honour. He has selected the chosen morsel and given it to him. He has shown him every possible embrace of trust and love and Judas's face goes dark, as shown in several of the great paintings of the Last Supper. Satan enters his soul and Jesus knows he is lost. That which we know will follow has now become inevitable and Jesus will not trample on his freedom to do it. We know that it was an act of generosity to Jesus with a box of precious ointment which led to Judas's initial betrayal, and here is an act of honouring generosity by Jesus that leads to the final treachery. The deeper we are in sin the more we hate the acts of generous love.

'What thou doest do more quickly', says Jesus, using the comparative to hurry him on. We can see the scene clearly as Judas slides past his former companions, guiltily lifts the latch of the door, and disappears into the dark. Christ's loneliness begins. He cannot tell his disciples. He cannot share his feelings with his friends. His Father, too, from now onwards, will gradually retreat into the blackness. All is lost as our final redemption begins. Darkness is the backcloth for every other scene of the drama.

John, the greatest playwright of Scripture, has two phrases that summarize the scenes and which sear their way into his readers' minds and souls. Later on are the five words, 'Now Barabbas was a robber', but even more piercing are his words to end Act V, scene I: 'And it was night.'

'But the light shines in the darkness and the darkness has never mastered it.'

17

The Cross – the Parable of Parables

The Cross and all that leads up to it is a practical business. It is no less than the rebuilding of a flawed world and the final bit of that rebuilding was done in seven days. More amazing still, the major part of that refurbishment was accomplished in twenty-four hours and the heart of the reconstruction in three.

The contention of this book is that the blueprint, the thinking behind that rebuilding is to be found principally in the parables. They display the mind of the maker. They are the closest that we get to Jesus's thinking on the issues that govern life and relationships and the theology undergirding all that Christ does and is. There are, of course, collected sayings such as the Sermon on the Mount. There are the discourses scattered through St John's Gospel, in which he, like Shakespeare, turns his hero's thoughts, words and character into the poetry of drama. And none the less genuine for that. But the place where I suspect we have the clearest and most authentic voice of our Lord is in those enigmatic stories.

Not only that, they are probably the parts of the Gospel where we can hear Jesus's voice and feel his personality and character leaping at us from the pages of the manuscript most clearly and powerfully. There are also his actions and interactions with people, seen through the eyes of the Gospel writers, but even those actions and interactions often have the nature of parable about them. Christ's emotions of joy, of compassion, his admiration of the ordinary person, his rebuke of the disciples and Jewish leaders, his love of the outsider and the wounded, take us into spheres of meaning that are akin to the parables. The healing of the man born blind in John, Chapter 9 is a wonderful example of parable lived out through an event involving all sorts of people.

The argument of this chapter is that the Cross and Passion are the summary of those parables, the silent exhibition of the theological thinking behind them. They are the early designs for the remodelling of creation. The essential lines of the drawings are found in those mysterious stories, and the last few days of our Lord's life lives out and builds what he has pictured in those glorious art forms. Never hesitant, as we have found, to use other people's ideas, but always twisting them into the shape required for the achievement of the work.

Jesus is the most risky of architects and having turned the accepted architectural values of the day upside down in the parables, he puts them into practice in the Passion. It must be so if a fallen, twisted and upside-down world is to be reconstructed as it was intended to be. If foolishness in the world's eyes is once again to be recognized as the wisdom of God. If, as Newman says in his hymn, Adam is to be rescued.

What are some of those values that shout at us from the parables and which the Cross summarizes in its amazing risk? Values that are also shouted at us from the Cross, in silence. Helpless silence it must be, because, above all, those values, those restored treasures, must be surrounded by, wrapped in, permeated by complete freedom. There must be no compulsion to buy when God displays his most precious wares. His advertisement not only leaves men and women free, it also frees them by its very nature. Just as the parables are perhaps the only way to teach and explore the nature of God without any form of compulsion, so the Cross is the only way to exhibit that nature in human flesh without any pressure that could rebind mankind. Not only is freedom the value that accompanies all other values, it also enables a fallen creation to embrace them as God would have us do.

Back to Adam. The first damage to God's world, we are told, was the loss of innocence symbolized by the knowledge of nakedness. The parable of the Garden of Eden is centred on that loss and the possibility of further damage by the consumption of fruit from the tree of life. Christ in his parables certainly restores an innocence and freshness to old tales, but it is through the parable of the Cross which takes place in complete nakedness that innocence is finally restored. R. S. Thomas says, 'A garden is God's gesture against the wild.' Through the nakedness of his soul before God in the Garden of Gethsemane and the nakedness of his love on the Cross, the world's wildness is tamed, innocence is reclaimed, Eden is restored. But in an upside-down way we are now invited to partake of the tree of life, life forever, as described in St John, Chapter 6. Again that flesh and blood is displayed in all its glory on the Cross. Moses, the Hebrew's greatest leader who was to lead them to the borders of the Eden of the Promised Land, was only allowed to see the back of God, no more would be possible. We now see our totally exposed God. The tree of the Cross is the tree of life.

Innocence and life are primary qualities in a restored universe, but life and innocence being what they are will require forgiveness for their continuance. Forgiveness must surround them. The parable of the Prodigal Son and the parable in Matthew, Chapter 18 are centred on forgiveness, and the father's forgiveness to the Prodigal restores innocence and life to the younger son. Both these parables display an utterly unconditional forgiveness. There are no terms, no small print (though such unconditionality is not accepted by the forgiven man in Matthew's parable).

Again, as I have described elsewhere, it is a reversal of the way the world usually forgives. Repentance, reparation, and a determination not to offend again are demanded by the Church and world. In the Old Covenant, too, compliance with the law, conformity to the ways of the community were required for restoration. (Certainly merciful by the standards of the time.) Nowadays the theological catch-all phrase, that there are no conditions attached to the offering of forgiveness, but there are of necessity conditions for its acceptance, does not appear in Christ's thinking, it would seem. Forgiveness in all its unconditional beauty is the 'renewable' clothes that innocence wears.

Likewise that other foundation of this total reconstruction – love. Foundation stones are by their nature hidden, and there are no parables specifically centred on the theme of love. The word is not mentioned in them. But love certainly pops up in not a few of them – the Good Samaritan, the Prodigal Son, the Good Shepherd. Love is hidden because that is the way with divine love. A total exposure of divine love would be so overwhelming, so compelling, that freedom to reject it would not be possible. God will not bully us into love. So it must be clothed in silence, clothed in disgrace if it is to make its appeal unconditionally. The radiance of divine love must be disguised if it is to tempt us freely.

One other foundation stone in this summary of the parables by means of the parable of the Cross. It is the foundation stone of powerlessness. Weakness is perhaps the wrong term, though it has the right flavour of gentleness, even if Christian thinking on this subject often looks to the world of power like unconvincing weakness. Christ's powerlessness is not a quality (for most) that refuses to defend even by force the weak, the innocent and those who cannot protect themselves. The powerlessness of God is not usually pacifism, though such thinking is a witness that needs to be there. The foundation stone of Christ's weakness, his powerlessness, is his utter refusal to align himself with anything, with any group that has final power of any sort over the destiny of their fellow men and women.

He flees at once when after the feeding of the 5000 as recorded in John's Gospel they try to take him by force to make him king. Jesus makes it clear by riding into Jerusalem on an ass that he is not coming as a conquering saviour. There is an utter refusal to use any power except that of love to protect himself from treachery or from what men would do to him. He could have allowed the disciples to restrain Judas from going out into the night. He could, according to Matthew, have called upon legions of angels at his trial, however metaphorical that may be. And the parables themselves are part of that type of powerlessness, with the nailed weakness of the Cross forming a summary of them. The depth of the simplicity of the parables in their telling rejects direct power in the phrase 'Those that have ears to hear, hear.' In other words, I am not forcing anything on you, but go away and think about it. See what it says about the nature of God. Perhaps at last some churches are by necessity beginning to probe more deeply into the powerlessness of Christ. Any institution, however, that considers itself a guardian of morals and orthodoxy and Church law, finds it almost impossible not to indulge in force of some kind. History is littered with the results. As Luther says, 'Associate religion with law and the latter will gain ground with the swiftness of an infectious disease.' The Cross advertises another way.

To use picture language again, what are the tools that our Lord employs to construct the new world through parable, and finally through the parable of his suffering? A veritable wealth of them: some sharp, some gentle, but nearly all unexpected. Let me mention but a few of them that other chapters have already illustrated and which are polished and made ready for human use by the Passion. First, the scandalous, which certainly goes hand in hand with the unexpected. The Unjust Judge and more boldly still the Unjust Steward are triumphantly such. Whatever the parables mean, both characters are acting scandalously. The judge gives in not from any desire to see justice done but because he can't take any more nagging. The steward cheats to ensure a comfortable future. Scandals are things that shock, that, as the word implies, mentally trip you up, are traps for the unwary, and Jesus uses this tool to break into minds, to challenge his hearers to dismiss surface thinking, so that they will penetrate into the depths behind the story.

As St Paul makes clear in the First Letter to the Corinthians, the Cross was the sharpest trip-stone of all. Set minds could not discern the mind of God behind such disgrace. They could not understand that this scandal was the key to the heart of God. The weakness of complete 'immoral' disgrace was the road to the Kingdom of Heaven. The only road back to innocence and life.

Risk and foolishness abound as further tools in this rebuilding process of the new world and humanity within it. The centre of risk is that you cannot control or know for certain the outcome of a particular course of action. There is no guarantee that the outcome will be as you hoped and planned. Add foolishness to that and you shorten still further the odds on the end being as you desired. Not only that, if foolishness as well is put into the risk your reputation will inevitably be at stake. God in Christ going down the road of scandalous, foolish risk as seen in the Cross is in severe danger of ending up with nothing to show for it and egg on the divine face.

Those are some of the incredible ingredients, the amazing tools, used for our salvation. Those are the levers used to turn creation the right way up again. And down the centuries generation after generation has tried to make Christian faith, morality and living respectable. Smother it with the thinking of the day. And time and time again the smothering has been on the surface successful. But in the end a naked, crucified, powerless blasphemer, according to the standards of the respectable of Christ's day (and often ours) can never be nailed down. Something which is respectable means that we have got it under control, blunted its edges, clothed it for the drawing room, so that we can wave it about in public without causing offence. We can, when it is not required for immediate use, pop it away in the wardrobe. But the parable of the crucified saviour doesn't fit into decent categories. Risk, scandal and foolishness lie at the heart of Christian theology and God requires followers who are also willing to be 'indecent' with painful humility. It is the way God has chosen to right his topsy-turvy world.

Somehow it was the indecency of the parables, their social and theological indecency, that seems to have attracted his audience and repelled many of the leaders of the day, though like voyeurs some of them couldn't resist being there. The parables cannot be tidied up and stored in cupboards for use as moral or doctrinal batons, though many preachers, politicians and priests have tried. They have thundered that this is what they mean and this is, therefore, how you will behave and how you will think. But they are indecently untidy stories. They are stories with scandalous beauty, like a Caravaggio painting perhaps. They are stories with foolish risk, and as untrappable as the Scarlet Pimpernel. They stand on the border between sharp reality and the depths of fearful mystery. They attract us to dig, to mine those lands of reality, and explore those oceans of dark enigma which border the Gospel shore. Likewise the Cross.

The parables turn normal thinking about forgiveness, punishment, reparation and thinly-disguised revenge upside down. They batter heart and mind, yet still leave people free. They explore and advertise the nature of God with both power and tenderness, yet never trap that nature or human nature in theological boxes. Likewise the Cross.

They parade the characteristics of Christ. His generosity, his extravagance, his crossing of boundaries that separate individuals and groups, his ability to penetrate and stand beside the despairing, the outcast, the unloved and the unlovable. Likewise the Cross.

The parables present us with the most ordinary and the deepest problems of our nature and God's being, and give us no easy answers or solutions. Instead they give us shoes for our pilgrim feet, and scents and signposts with which to hunt our divine quarry, with all the excitements and despairs that the chase will provide. Likewise the Cross.

18

The Good Samaritan

St Luke 10: 25–37

Songs and sayings that excite the heart! There's a title for a book! History is littered with such music and such words. Many that still stir us, open doors into excitement, inspire us to do great or little deeds, use our talents, unclick our purses, and love our neighbour. Down the ages from Joshua to Churchill, from the psalms to football matches, men and women have been inspired by a phrase, released by a sentence, lifted by the music of words.

For Christians the source book is the Bible and their service books. The prophets, the psalms, proverbs, the poetry of St Paul, leap out at us, enable us to feel the excitement of their first use, and make it our own. We do the same with Shakespeare. We use such phrases unconsciously, not knowing their origin. Such are the engineers of our souls.

But our Lord is the master, the maestro of the art. Distilling into a few words excitements and power that have moved worlds, caused revolutions, inspired individuals and communities to heroism, and given supposed authority to those who wish to burn and slaughter their religious neighbours. Most of us can conjure them up almost without a thought. 'You cannot serve God and mammon.' 'The first shall be last and the last shall be first.' 'Render unto Caesar the things that are Caesar's and unto God the things that are God's.' Though most of us would be hard pushed to know exactly what that meant. Let me take one which at first reading doesn't seem to cheer, excite, hit us between the frontal lobes, or make the heart beat faster but which in fact, it seems to me, destroys enough chains to unshackle much of humanity. It is this: 'The Sabbath was made for man not man for the Sabbath.' Hardly earth-shattering people might say, but I would suggest the phrase has the power to unlock the door to a library of thinking. Hidden within it is at least part of the parable of the Good Samaritan.

You remember the scene? The disciples strolling through the cornfields with Jesus on the Sabbath day. Listening to the master, being taught the excitements of the Kingdom of God, and anyone, as they walked and talked, would pluck a few ears, extract the grain, and have a chew or two. But that is reaping and threshing – forbidden on the Sabbath. It was the authorities' 'alien corn', *verboten*, against the grain. In other words, the law about the Sabbath which was meant to release people for a rest-day, for joy and restoration, had become a bondage. Instead of the law freeing people to enjoy a day of ease, instead of the law being a releasing gift of God, it had enslaved them to pettiness. Even such things as the number of stitches you could sew on the Sabbath was fixed. Carrying a chair with too many struts in the back was considered akin to carrying a ladder and not allowed. The lawyers claimed it made life easier because simple folk then knew where they stood, but not only did it chain them, it gave the authorities power over them and that led to fear. Behind the lawyer's question lay the same sort of thinking. Who was or was not your neighbour was stated in the law, surely that was the end of the matter.

Jesus is the great releaser from fear of the petty, from fear of people and regulations. He is the freer of those who are captured by some form of so-called Christian faith, captured when they had wished to fly and serve their Lord. Jesus's revolutionary dictum about the Sabbath is saying that commandments were made for man not man for commandments, and they are, therefore, relative, and temporary. They are there to free us and as soon as they cease to free persons and communities they must go. And all that spills over surely into morality.

But it can go further than that. It can work the other way too. Plenty of men and women think that if they have not broken the commandments, the rules, the laws of Church and state, they are righteous, justified. They think as well that those who have broken a rule or law in however petty a way are less worthy than they. Some of the nastiest people I have known have never broken the ten commandments, have never broken the speed limit, have never driven with more than 81mg of alcohol in their blood, have never been a neighbour from hell.

We have often on our streets and in our institutions been guilty of equating the peace of legalism with goodness. Control by the power of law with stability. As the German philosopher Fichte says, 'I would prefer an injustice to a disorder', and at heart most authorities would agree with him. But the necessity of such a saying is usually the result of tyranny, and also the way to more of it. Jesus makes clear that there is another way and makes it clear in this parable. The choice between injustice and disorder should be unnecessary.

I realize, of course, that there are no complete answers to this problem, and we must distinguish order (rather than orders) from quietness by commandment control. The beginning of Genesis is about the beauty created from chaos by order. Chaos turned into creation and creativity. The author of Psalm 119 is using those words such as law, statute, order, testimony, commandment (he uses them in every verse in the psalm except three) as a yearning for the establishment of the beauty of order. Luke's Gospel gives us a picture of a Lord who revels in the beauty of the freedom of order. Matthew is much more of a control-by-commandment man.

In a Church, in the Kingdom of the Gospel, in a free land there will be limits beyond which, for the good of the community, it is unwise and dangerous to stray. Sin often abounds! But morality in many of its forms is relative, and once it becomes absolute we are in for danger too. There is more than a hint of this in Jewish authority figures in the Gospels. 'It is expedient that one man should die for the people, rather than that the whole nation should be destroyed', says Caiaphas. Back to Fichte perhaps. And there is a smell of it, the binding by commandment, in the questioner who provoked the parable of the Good Samaritan. Once you put what you suppose is your duty to God in conflict with your duty to mankind, as it seems the Levite and priest did, you are in real danger and so is everybody else. Or to put it another way, once you start putting your 'faith' higher than your God, compassion and much else goes out of the ecclesiastical window.

All of which means risks have to be taken. Personal risks, community risks. At times a risk because you think that people have large chunks of inherent goodness hidden in them, waiting to be released by freedom. Rather than constantly thinking that we are inherently evil through and through, and then legislating for this in Church and state. Theological risks must be taken, even with what the Church considers is the nature of God. This is presumably what Jesus was talking about when he risked the theology of the Sabbath.

Again that is what the Cross stands for. It came about because Jesus trespassed the bounds of the theology that lay behind the law. Breaking the Sabbath was trespassing on areas that they thought had something to do with the nature of God. Breaking purity rules likewise. Jesus might well have said to Levite and priest 'Purity rules were made for man, not man for the purity rules'. Again and again the exclusivity boundaries of the Jewish faith (pictured in this parable) were crossed by our Lord and the authorities couldn't take it.

One rider before I deal with the parable, and then only briefly. A rider that is not a retraction. Despite all I have said I still think a framework to our thinking and our doing is necessary. We must have our boundaries. A form is needed for our thoughts and our behaviour. I am not a total anarchist. Bach and Mozart and many others wrote their most profound, most beautiful, harmonically free and risky music within a strict framework, fugal form, sonata form and so on. They were ordered but not chained. I rest my case.

Thoughts around the Parable

Whenever anybody not well-up in the Gospel narratives is asked in a quiz a question about the parables, the inevitable answer trotted out is the Good Samaritan. And, mind you, they are usually right. Perhaps those who set quizzes don't know any other parables either. The Good Samaritan probably has more connotations for this and that in secular life than any other. Politicians use it to justify their remarks on social policy, and on colour, class and creed. For plain beauty it takes some beating. Not a word wasted, every phrase crafted. Like the parable on forgiveness it was told in response to a question. Was it, therefore, spontaneous or was it an adaptation of a local story, or had Jesus considered such matters already and thought out his stories for such occasions?

In essence it is the simplest of stories. You can picture every bit of it and frame the painting with imagination. And the same could be said about the Passion narrative. Both this parable and the Passion are about journeys, about rejection and about wounds. About a journey to Jericho, across the rugged wilderness. About a journey to Golgotha along the rugged way of pain and forsakenness. About abandoned victims on a journey. Authoritarian figures are involved along the way for both travellers. Priest and Levite, Herod, Pilate, the soldiers and Pharisees. Rejection in both cases by those who represent the faith. Hidden within this parable are constant reminders of the Passion.

St Augustine of Hippo couldn't resist turning the whole thing into an allegory. In brief outline, for Augustine the Samaritan is Christ who brings wounded mankind to the Church represented by the inn, the two pence given to the innkeeper are the two sacraments of baptism and communion (part of Passiontide), and the phrase 'Whatever more I owe you I will repay when I return' is the second coming of Christ. All beautifully done. Like the Prodigal Son this parable has the beauty of major and minor keys that moves hearts and minds in anger, in joy and in thoughtfulness.

It is a risky parable too. Most obviously the risk to Christ himself, another nail in his Cross. He delivers in this story a straightforward attack on much that controlled the standards of Jewish life. Purity laws in particular. Road crossing or not doing so is the centre-piece of the tale, as it is in so many ways with the Passion. Let me do a St Augustine on that story in another way.

On his journey to the Cross and beyond, barriers are crossed either by Jesus or by those he contacts. Barriers of just about every kind. The barrier of criminality in the penitent thief. Of family distinctions, as Mary becomes John's mother and he her son. Even those old enemies Pilate and Herod are reconciled for a while. They meet in the middle of the power road. And the reconciliation that Christ effects in the end doesn't blur differences, it enables them to be embraced and beatified. No doubt you sing that hymn from time to time that contains the line 'And the colour and the creed and the class don't matter'. I realize what the writer means and in the sense he uses the phrase clearly he is right. But those things matter desperately because they are all part of a person's make-up. They are gifts or accidents from God. Skin colour certainly is. It is part of a person's glory. They matter enormously, but they have to cease to be barriers and become things of unity and joy instead, and because that is so, they have to be healed and redeemed by the divine road-crosser. The Samaritan and the wounded Jew remained a Samaritan and a Jew after the road-crossing, but they were united through wounding. Such is our Lord's work. All a very risky business, as Northern Ireland and elsewhere bear witness.

The parable also has the glory of incompleteness about it. Incomplete work. It starts with a question and ends with one. It is a take-away parable. Work out in your daily lives who your neighbour is and then act accordingly. The whole Passion is a working-out of that, and an unresolved one. Is Judas still Christ's neighbour? Is the impenitent thief? Does Peter cease to be Christ's neighbour after his triple betrayal? Again, what does all that mean for us and our impenitence and our betrayals?

To continue in this questioning style, it is not only a matter of crossing the road but what do we do when we get to the other side? We are all famous in one way or other for doing a cowboy job with our acts of charity. Doing enough to still our consciences but never completing the job. Pouring in wine and oil, patting the wounded man on the head, and then waving goodbye. After all, we have other acts of charity to perform further down the road and a religious service to attend.

There is the famous story of George Herbert, an Anglican priest at the beginning of the seventeenth century, who arrived at a meeting of clergy late and covered in mud. His fellow priests were aghast but he just made his apologies and left it at that. It transpired that he had spent a long time pulling a poor man and his cart out of the ditch and then seeing him to his destination. Task completed.

Although the Passion is complete in the details of the action, it is always incomplete. Christ expects us to carry on his Passiontide work. St Paul has a mysterious passage which he puts into the sort of phrase I began this chapter with. 'I am completing what still remains for Christ to suffer.' We are expected to join Christ in his work which is, in time, ever incomplete.

Just two other things about the priest and Levite. I doubt whether they were evil men. Religion can become so compartmentalized that we do not see certain things as our job. Compassion was not their job. Other things took precedence. How often have people passed by those being attacked in the streets or have passed by a car accident? 'It's not my job to get involved,' we say, 'there are others specially qualified to do that. I must get back to my family.' And my second excuse for the priest and Levite, who represent the official Church, is that they are loaded with historical chains.

Not a logical working out of the parable but a few thoughts. It is that sort of parable. It is very much a 'feelings' parable. A parable that should affect and change our emotions and passions. I wonder if there weren't a degree of impulsiveness about the Good Samaritan. 'Blow to convention, I'm going to see what's up,' he says. And there are times when that must be our style in beauty, in risk and practice. There are times when the paint must be splashed recklessly on the charity canvas. There is an inspired, thought-out recklessness about Christ's Passion. Every move devised, yet there is no guarantee that he will come out the other side of death. He takes the ultimate risk and dices with the devil, playing the game with total skill and artistry. There is a magnetic masterpiece in it all that compels us to follow our Lordly Good Samaritan. It proclaims – 'Go and do thou likewise.'

19

Three More Parables

St Matthew 25

Matthew gives us a wonderfully contrasting set of parables immediately before the Passion story begins, and all mainly centred on a
couple of themes: surprise and judgement, with much else thrown in
for the delight of the hearers, such as responsibility for what is
entrusted to us, such as the realization that Jesus is hidden in his
people, particularly the poor and needy, and a swipe at the religious
leaders of his day.

First, before I go off on something tangential to these parables,
a word again about our Lord's living-out of the main themes of these
stories: judgement and surprise. Judgement first. He is certainly harsh
with those who prevent the ordinary people from coming close to
God. He finds certain attitudes abhorrent such as pretence at piety
and Scroogery with riches. He suggests that those who isolate themselves from the poor and despised are in danger of a sticky eternity.
But with people who come to him having committed moral offences
or having been involved in immorality of various kinds he is gentle
and compassionate. He would have found some Victorians difficult
to embrace.

He warns, too, about being judgemental. We are assured that
Christ will come to judge the quick and the dead, but the judge of all
is seldom condemnatory and is quick with mercy in both senses of
the word 'quick'. Yes, he puts the terror of judgement in front of his
hearers, but he is not judgemental.

But the whole feel of this Lord and master of parables is one of
delightful surprise. It is one of his most entrancing characteristics,
life-giving surprise. It permeates not only his telling of the parables,
but the parables themselves. From the first word, whether they be

original or borrowed, they are instilled with quickening attractiveness. They are compelling, however many times we have heard them, and they have a freshness that never needs dusting. They always have a twist, a surprise. They always have an unexpectedness. They always reveal something new about the workings of the 'God of surprises'. And that surprise, that twist, that unexpectedness, that novelty is at the centre of the Gospel itself.

The Good News may build on the history and prophets of Israel, but the bricks that Christ uses from the Old Testament construct a new and ever 'a-gasping' building, designed and furnished in an unexpectedly new way. Such architecture eventually overwhelmed his own world and threatens our own with its beauty and unexpectedness.

Secondly, in the run-up to these parables, something about the meaning of the little word 'brethren' used in the parable of the Sheep and the Goats, plus some thoughts leading on from that word. And in this case it is not just a matter of academic semantics. Scholarly theologians differ about whether the word 'brethren' here and elsewhere in the New Testament is a confining word or not. That's the crux. Does brethren mean anybody, anywhere, Christians and non-Christians, or does it mean that we are judged by our response to those who are our brethren in the faith and those alone?

Are we judged by our charity to the sick, poor, and imprisoned who are our fellow Christians, and not by our charity to outsiders? Certainly Matthew has a very Jewish community feel to his Gospel. The keeping of the law and almost the containment of the Christian faith within it, is strongly felt. So is it a parable about goodness to all, or goodness to believers?

Certainly in St John's First Letter, particularly Chapters 2 and 3, the emphasis is very much on our fellow Christians as the target for charity and harsh judgement. There is a feel that the world outside the community of faith hardly exists except as a temptation to be avoided by the followers of Christ. Mind you, in the first two or three centuries of the faith to do anything else but be a palisade-surrounded Church was almost impossible – so sharp were the lines of division between Christians and the state religion, so fierce were the persecutions. Grey areas of any kind in doctrine and practice were not possible. Parts of the New Testament are bound to reflect this. I suspect the last parable of the group does so.

One last point before we look at the parables themselves:

immediacy. All the Gospels, particularly Mark's, have a feeling of breathlessness about them. Jesus is in a rush. Time is short, things must be done straight away, directly, immediately. He has all the time in the world for people, but time is short for preaching, teaching and for the world itself. This feeling of living in the last times, of the immediacy of the second coming, a feeling present in the first and last of these parables, was taken over by the early Church.

St Paul in his early letters, particularly those to the Thessalonians, suggests that the Lord will return in his lifetime, but by the time his later letters appear, and certainly by the time the Gospels were written, the feeling of living as if the end were near was still the expectation, even if its immediacy was less certain. There was an urgency of his coming that governed the nature of actions, rather than the certainty of its happening next Wednesday. In other words, the early Church became gradually less certain about the second coming arriving soon, but more certain that the possibility of that coming should govern the course of our actions and thinking. These parables penned after Paul and most of the apostles were dead also have that feeling about them. It wasn't that living under judgement had been moved to the not-so-pending file but that it was ever here in spirit, even if God had delayed the coming of the divine meteorite.

And such has been the theology of the Church down the ages even at its most tired. St Ignatius Loyola said, as have many others, 'Live as if you were going to die tomorrow. Die as if you were going to live for ever'. Bishop Thomas Ken of Bath and Wells in his morning hymn 'Awake my soul', says 'Redeem thy misspent time that's past, and live each day as if thy last. Improve thy talent with due care, for the great day thyself prepare.' He clearly had the middle parable of the Talents in mind. Vigilance of the kind found in the first parable features in a Bach cantata or two. We are expected to live under judgement's shadow. One terrifying meaning of the word 'repent' in classical Greek, the same word used for 'repent' by the Gospel writers, is 'to change your mind when it is too late'. The parable of the Ten Virgins has that scent of sulphur about it.

The Parables

Matthew carefully places these masterpieces immediately before the Passion narrative. They are almost part of it. The Cross and Passion judge the world and transform it with tender mercy. These parables face us with some of the characteristics of that judgement. Perhaps the surprising fact about those yardsticks of judgement is that the accent is always as much, if not more, on what we failed to do as on what we did. Sins of omission have that added appallingness of blindness and insensitivity. Jesus found lack of awareness very difficult to stomach, it seems. Sins of lack of recognition which are central to the parable of the Sheep and the Goats are central to the trial of Jesus in Jerusalem. His judges, both sacred and secular, the mockers and the baying crowd, failed utterly to recognize their Lord. Only the centurion perhaps was aware of his origin.

I find it significant that Jesus nearly always talks about judgement and its unexpectedness in stories, in parables. Unlike the prophets, who although they use vivid images at times, pound their hearers with the terrors and sudden arrival of it in direct terms. There is a note of anger about them. Jesus chooses to use extended music, rather than just the words of a *dies irae* to penetrate our souls more subtly.

First, a brief word about the three parables. It used to be thought that with the parable of the Ten Virgins Matthew had turned the whole thing into an allegory and there was no evidence for believing that bridegrooms arrived and feasted in the middle of the night, or that there were torchlight processions. Now, however, opinion has changed. Lamp-lighting was common in our Lord's day and as usual he is describing the actual. Allegory it may be, with Christ as the bridegroom, the Christian community as the wise virgins, and Israel the foolish ones, but the excitement of the occasion, the terror of not being admitted still comes through. You can see the lights that shine on the face of the bridegroom and the flames of the torches of judgement.

The second parable has none of the excitement of the Ten Virgins or the seeming simplicity of the Sheep and the Goats. In Luke's version it is a singularly unpleasant story and it is generally considered that Matthew's version is earlier and closer to the original. Even here it is an odd and slightly rancid filling in this three-parable sandwich, but again, judgement is swift and judgement strangely harsh. The early Church, and 'Matthew' himself, would have allegorized the merchant's journey as the Ascension of Christ, and his sudden reappearance as the *parousia* (the second coming), where he scatters rewards and in this case a double punishment – forfeiture and tossing into eternal darkness. Keeping the riches of God's word from the ordinary people, the buried talent incurs Christ's anger especially.

And again, with an abrupt change of scene, Matthew takes us from grinding teeth to the standard picture of the second coming at the start of the third parable. Thrones and angels with trembling nations in front of our Lord. Then with equal abruptness the judgemental electricity is earthed with the familiar scene of the Sheep and the Goats. We are back on a Jesus-type painting. Back on the genuine canvas.

As his hearers would have known, the Palestinian shepherd separates goats from sheep at night for the goats are more fragile and need warmth. The sheep are tougher and more valuable. Added to which is the colour difference. White being the colour of righteousness. Then comes the wonderfully told parable beloved of preachers in theory and of many of the saints in practice. St Hugh of Lincoln and Edward King of Lincoln, for instance, both rejoiced to feed the poor and visit those in prison. It has superb little touches such as the surprise of both those who displayed charity and mercy and those who didn't. 'Lord when was it . . . ?' Charity must have that sort of innocence about it, if it is to reflect and contain the divine, and lack of it has a disregard and a blindness which is often more chilling than the sin itself.

So where do the categories of judgement lie? Certainly in our alertness to the presence of Christ, to his coming. I have already written about the state of mind that prompts us to live as if the *parousia* is round the corner. The preparedness that our souls are repentedly ready to meet our Lord today. The Church sets aside seasons for such preparedness, but all Christian feasts and seasons, happy or penitential, are only concentrations, focuses, for what should be our remembrance all the time. Easter may last in undiluted form for forty days, but our alertness to the new life should permeate every minute of the year, unconsciously most of the time. All Saints' Day focuses us on the example and prayers of those godly men and women, but their names should be written on our signposts all the year and alert our souls.

Jesus had that alertness, combined with quickness of thought and action that shouts at us from every page of the Gospels. He is ready to deal with every situation as his Father would have done. He adored those from every nation with that brightness, that wit, that ready humility, such as the Syro-Phoenicean woman and the centurion who came asking for favours. It is our ability to be ready to find Christ the bridegroom in every situation, in every person that Jesus expects from us and enjoys from us. Light us with the oil of grace as our allegory-man might say. Failure to be ready gets door-slamming treatment in the parable and the possibility that it can happen finally perhaps.

And similar to that is our failure to see that lack of charity is not only failure to our fellow men and women but failure to Christ himself. To the image of Christ imprinted in the poor, the sick, the imprisoned. Hidden in all creation is the Creator, and we genuflect to our Lord in service and love in that hiddenness. Shouting also from that parable is simplicity. They are wonderfully simple acts of charity: feeding the hungry, giving drinks to the thirsty, visiting the sick and imprisoned. We are judged by our response to the cries of the ordinary, not necessarily by our patriotism or our outstanding courage or our banner-waving evangelism. The Gospel is full of our Lord's profound simplicity.

The middle parable is also about failure by the Jewish leaders to open up the riches of God. They hid the treasures that had been entrusted to them by God and would in the end be answerable to him. Not only that, those riches, the parable makes clear, would eventually be given to others who had shown themselves responsible in handling the pearls of God. The history of all faiths is littered with locked chests, hidden riches, storehouses of gospel, where only those with the right password can have possession. The same is true of all knowledge which confers power. Medicine, government, law and so on. Those in charge of such areas have time and time again protected their information so that they can control others. Failure in our openness with gifts and the responsibilities that they give us, make us answerable to a saddened God, whose sadness is more terrifying than his sword.

And all those failures are gathered up by the Cross and Passion of Christ. Failures of recognition, failure to embrace the simplicity of Christ's love and care, failure with the use of power. St Luke in his parable of the Talents uses the same word for the cloth surrounding the buried talent as he does for the grave-cloth surrounding the head of Christ in the tomb. The only times that particular word is used in the New Testament. Meditationally, it seems to me that even in death the riches of his mind are wrapped and buried in an attempt to prevent them from exploding into a waiting world.

In the end it is the ordinariness of the failures which is the most frightening thing of all. No wonder Judgement Day may be most fearsome if it come not with a bang but with a whimper.